Printed in Poland by Amazon

First Printing, 2019

ISBN 9781795314435

Via Paganora 21,
25121 Brescia
Italy

www.Patient-Acquisition.com

ONLINE PATIENT ACQUISITION SECRETS

The Underground Playbook to Double Your Patients Overnight

MAX ARNAUDO

www.patient-acquisition.com

Table Of
CONTENTS

FOREWORD

I f you're reading this book, chances are you're into acquiring patients.

Whether for you, your hospital, or your products, all these valuable strategies apply. The insights in this book are worth thousands of dollars. Most of this information is actually sold for thousands of dollars by marketing experts all over the world.

I'm happy you're holding this book in your hands, whether it's due to the dollars you'll save by not giving your business to an incompetent agency or due to the insights you'll gain for driving your marketing decisions.

As of the time of this writing, our agency has grossed millions of dollars (and euros) for our customers. Some of them are dentists, others are surgeons. We also work with hospitals, physical products (from pharma to toothbrushes), and services in the health world. Everywhere the word "patient" applies, we have been studying the psychology and processes, the things that make their minds tick, and the underlying technology that makes it happen. We started as an agency but we're rapidly evolving into a healthcare network.

It's staggering; I feel that, in the health world, most business efforts focus on useless processes. Hospitals buy expensive machinery because their admins are sold into believing they're "the best machines." Consequently, they end up with a low marketing budget.

However, if your patients don't know that you're "the best," it won't help that you've spent millions of dollars on the best equipment. Broadcasting your message and content to a thousand more people a day would have a bigger overall impact and a larger and faster return on investment.

The good thing about digital marketing is that you can measure what you're doing. We can track how much you've spent and how much you've earned as a result.

This book might contain some occasional grammar errors (English is not my first language), and I hope you'll forgive us for that. I hope that the value in these words will overcome what your grammar teacher might think about them.

This book is not for someone who is interested in debating "ethics." I assume that you're an honest person, that you don't over-treat your patients to increase your profits, and that you will follow all your profession's guidelines when following this advice. I like to talk about money, but this doesn't mean I don't expect you to do your job while keeping your patients' health in mind.

If you're a dentist, you don't install implants that you wouldn't want in yourself. If you manage a hospital, it's the type of hospital where you'd want your family to recover. And so on. I won't debate whether it's right to acquire patients on an industrial scale; if you're sure that you are a great professional, then you deserve more patients and more patients deserve you.

My goal is for you to apply the strategies in this book and to profit from them. These are real strategies, and somebody is already calling me a fool for releasing them like this, in a book, when they available are on the market for very high prices.

Don't apply these strategies at your risk and peril. In this book, you'll learn how your profession is changing. How unstoppable forces are reshaping the way you work and communicate. Not heeding them would have you see the same end as those of Nokia, Encarta Encyclopedias, and Blockbuster. The same revolutions you see in everyday life—e.g., using Netflix instead of renting DVDs at Blockbuster—affect your profession too. The first businesses taking advantage of it are profiting immensely. Whoever wakes up late won't be that lucky.

Apply these strategies alone and see your professional and personal lives change. People will recognize you when you dine in a restaurant. Your lifestyle will change. You'll be more confident, just as anybody in control of their economic life is. You'll be more relaxed as you'll have a system that automatically brings a constant flow of patients to your door.

My wish is that this advice will benefit not only you but also your employees and loved ones.

Let's do it.

Max Arnaudo

Patient-Acquisition.Com

CHAPTER 1

Where is the money?

What is working now, and why you can't continue doing what used to work

H ere's how this story starts: I have been selling stuff on the internet since I was 19. But "stuff" is stuff. It's products. I would never have imagined that we would end up selling dental implants at this magnitude. I didn't ever imagine having hospitals call us asking us to advertise their businesses. But let's start from the beginning.

If you studied at medical school, manage a clinic or sell a product aimed at patients, there's something you probably share with me: You are a very stubborn person.

I have sold all kinds of stuff on the internet, especially bikinis. One day I ended up helping a friend promote his clinic online. We were just talking and he said, "Hey, if you can sell anything, would you be able to promote dental implants online for me?"

Challenge accepted. We brainstormed for weeks. At the time, I was new to this but we had dozens of friends in healthcare at every level: surgeons, doctors, dentists, etc.

The first campaigns we ran went horribly. When I say "horribly," I mean we got somebody to write us a few appointments. That was it. I wasn't happy with the copy, the images, or what we were offering. I could sense there was a huge potential, but I didn't know at what level.

If you're reading this book, chances are you like to play the game even when the evening has come, when your team has gone home, when you're still thinking of ways to improve your business.

If you're reading this book, you're probably not playing the eight-hours-a-day/five-days-a-week game. We're playing the same game.

This game keeps me awake at night. We play it with the same focus we used on games when we were children. The same focus a teenager uses to play video games. When I start speaking about the opportunities we have now with digital marketing, I become a child again. Why? Because the opportunities are huge.

If you're reading this book, we're similar because when I have a problem, I seek help in books, in people, in my team. If you're a health professional and you're reading a book on how to acquire more patients, chances are you'll acquire more.

Back in the day, online campaigns didn't work, yet I still had a sixth sense that they could. Online works with everything. I have friends acquiring clients for law firms. If it works for a law firm, it must work for patients, I thought.

For two to three months, I closed myself up at home (not even in my office, where I would have faced too many distractions). I got to know people doing my job in the UK and the USA and consulted with them because I wanted to know how this could possibly work. It became sort of an obsession.

At the moment of this writing, we generate millions in patients acquired every month. When one of my clients acquires four patients for $25.000 each, he grosses $100.000 in one month, with only our services. If you multiply that for our clients in Europe and overseas, we happily reach millions a month fast.

Acquiring patients changed my life. You might expect a technical book, and much of the knowledge that I share here is technical. However, you'll see that what makes our campaigns work is an understanding of how a patient's mind works. How it works online.

I have acquired this knowledge and I share it with my team every day. Together, my clients, my team and I profit thanks to the opportunities of online patient acquisition. In this book, we'll dive into them. Come get the secrets.

The secrets

In the beginning, there was SEO: Search Engine Optimization. You fill your website with words about what you do and your website gets to the first page on Google.

Cool, right? Billions of dollars have passed through SEO in the health world. There were many kinds of SEO:

- Good SEO created by professionals with white-hat techniques. (These are techniques that apply to Google policies. Remember the term white-hat, as it means you're a good guy. When you receive emails from Arabian princesses asking to share their $500 million inheritance, that is still online marketing, but black-hat.)

- Bad SEO guys cheating the Google algorithm and achieving great results, but only in the short term. These are the guys who called you one day and told you that Google f*cked them. You could still have made good money with them.

- Bad SEO guys, big or little agencies, looking to sell you a 12- to 24-month plan for a service you don't need and that they can't provide.

Speaking about SEO in 2018 has little point to you, to me or to anybody in the health world. Anybody pricing you SEO services, <u>especially for generic keywords,</u> is probably trying to f*ck you. I urge you to contact me on social media if you're having results with them. I'll make a case out of it. I don't mean if you had results with them, i mean if you are having results today in 2019, in healthcare, for generic keywords.

SEO used to work, and it can still work. Today people can travel the world riding a donkey, but that doesn't mean you should do it (unless you really love donkeys, right?).

Why not SEO anymore?

Once upon a time, during the first days and years of Google, if you bought the keyword "dentist new york" on Google, you'd buy a space that clearly looked like an ad.

I mean, due to its different color and "sponsored message" layout, it was clear that what you'd clicked on was an ad.

Back in the days the above line of text: "Ads related to Australian 100 Series 3 Burner Gas BBQ" made it clear to uncle Tom that he was clicking on an ad, and not on a real, organic result. The ads used to have a orange or green background that had them stand out.

On the internet, looking like an ad is ALWAYS a bad idea.

Something I always try to pass along to my clients is: People don't like ads. Our ads should never look like ads. Our ads should look like stories, like news, like something a friend is sharing.

Platforms like Google and Facebook know this, so they now offer services called "native." Native means that the ad doesn't look like an ad, but like something native to the platform. This is the reason why big, evident ads on Google now look almost identical to organic, real search results.

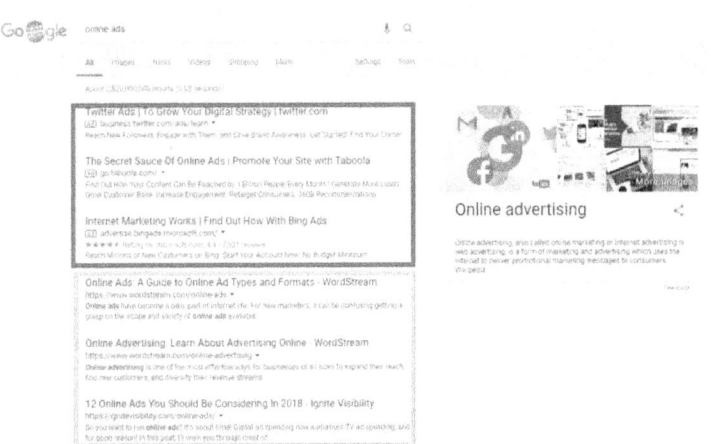

Today spotting the difference between an ad and an organic results got difficult, and poor uncle Tom gets easily fooled !

I need to repeat this because it has to be clear for you to understand this chapter: If you pay for Google Ads now, you'll get a result that tastes and looks like organic. This means that if I buy a keyword and bid high enough for it to appear on your screen, it will be VERY DIFFICULT for you to determine whether the result is real or an ad. Buying a keyword on Google means that anybody doing that research will see our ad. So, if you bought "dentist new york," we can assume that, depending on your budget, people searching for that term would have seen your ad.

The fact that it was an ad was very evident years ago.

Back then, you got "obviously ads" results, and then real, organic, chosen-by-Google results.

People trust the real results more than they the "ad" results. The majority of people used to scroll down and clicked on the real, organic results that Google was suggesting (not the ones that Google was paid to showcase).

Some people clicked on the first sponsored ad, but that traffic isn't the best traffic. If you work in advertising and have ever bought traffic (e.g., buying people's attention on the web, buying fluxes of people surfing on the web), you know how **"intent"** is important.

Intent: the intention an user has before actually clicking on an ad. Somebody searching for "smartphones" has a different intent than somebody searching for "Iphone"

If somebody is looking for Dacia cars and you show them Toyota, they might be interested a bit, but they were expressly looking for Dacia and they'll eventually look for that site. If I go to a grocery store and ask for carrots, I want carrots. Yes, the grocery man can try to sell me some spinach, too. It's still a grocery item, but I'm there for carrots.

I'm telling you this in case you think that you'll get profitable campaigns by buying your competitor's name. This can work, but it's not the smartest move. You can do it as a corollary to a complex online marketing campaign. However, if that is your spearhead: Houston, we have a problem.

Now, SEO impacts the real, organic results. What happens now is that, if you live in a city with a decent number of people (let's say, everywhere except the Himalayas or the Russian steppe), the first four to six results will be paid ones.

I'll say this again: When you do SEO for a keyword that has enough competitiveness to interest somebody else who is not you, you will have to share your space with many other websites. And these websites are going to show up way before you do.

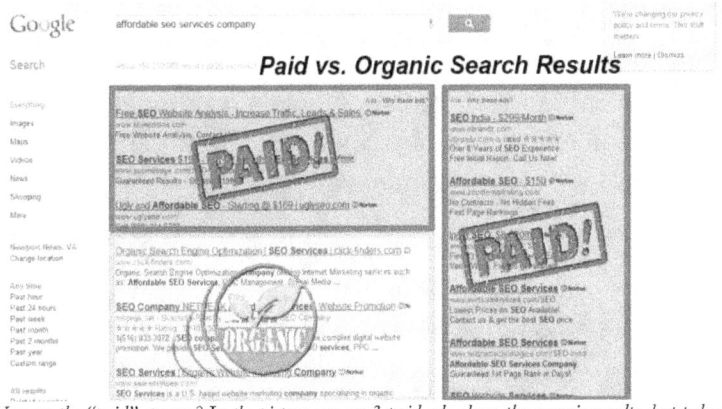

You see the "paid" spaces ? In the picture you see 3 paid ads above the organic results, but today they can reach up to 5-6, so that the "organic" results will be shown low low low. When you do SEO you can only affect the organic results. You can be the best at SEO but your website will be always be shown below the paid ads. The paid ads are taking up always more space, and they are now looking the same as organic results.
Not a good news for SEO guys.

So, when your SEO guy tells you, "YEAH, WE'RE FIRST PAGE WITH YOUR KEYWORD!," you need to think, *Ok, buddy, we're first page, but actually one has to go through four results in paid ads and another three on a map before reaching us.* That, in internet terms, it's a lot.

It's like you're looking for cheese at a supermarket. If you sell cheese, would you like your cheese to be on the first shelf or the bottom one? Would you accept having your cheese at the back of the supermarket? Or maybe inside a box, hidden somewhere close to the ice cream?

Somebody once said: The best place to find a dead body is the second page of Google.

That's because nobody EVER goes there. I mean, how many times, when you're searching for something on the internet, do you surf to page 2, 3 or 4 on Google? You simply don't. When you're not happy, you rephrase the search.

You can hide a dead body on page 2 and nobody will ever find it. You can smell a dead body at the end of page 1 because nobody checks the last results of page 1, either.

When, in this book, I talk about numbers I often say "nobody" or "everybody." When one considers that we're working with large numbers of people (traffic) surfing the web and striving every day to catch their attention, the term "everybody" means 93-98% of these people. That's enough.

We live in an age of fast thinking and fast reading. People, especially on the internet, want answers FAST. You don't want to spend the day navigating the web looking for a dentist. You want a dentist to be suggested to you when you speak to your friend about dentists. That's exactly why online ad spending is moving from Google to Facebook (and also why you feel that sometimes your phone is spying on you, but we'll talk about that later).

Long story short: You can't expect to make money using the same techniques people were making a profit from 10 years ago. My grandfather built houses in Italy in the 1960s and 1970s. Am I building houses, too? NO. If you build houses in Italy now, you get burned. Everyone knows it (Unless it's for some tourism thing maybe, but real estate isn't doing well in southern Europe since 2008).

I'm not building houses in Italy, and you shouldn't be investing lots of money in SEO in 2018. SEO guys will be mad at me for saying this, but it's the truth. It's written here in this book and on our clients' balance sheets, black on white.

I urge you to find an SEO agency that hasn't moved to other forms of advertising. Again: I know people have achieved good results with SEO. However, please note my use of the past tense "achieved." You need what works now.

You need something that is easier than SEO. Something over which you have more control and that is not completely outsourced in a 36-month project.

The psychology of SEO and of Google paid search

Somebody clicking on your Google Ads while looking for "dentist new york" doesn't know: Anything about you

Anything about your practice

Anything about anything

This person is probably among the worst potential patients you can have.

These are the patients who write "price" under a Facebook post or who call your secretaries asking for, again, price.

Although price is essential and anyone who asks about it is not necessarily interested only in that, you (and I) know that better patients are out there.

What if you could have all your patients always post about your clinic on Facebook after they visit you? How many of their friends would be informed about it?

What if somebody could read all the information he needs to read, all the information about you and your story, all on one page BEFORE they call you?
Damn, it's psychology. It's the patient journey.

What content am I feeding my patient BEFORE she makes a decision?

And again, is that content easily accessible, or it is distributed on a website containing 100 pages, with theoretical/professional language, made by a doctor for a doctor rather than by a doctor for a patient?

Remember one thing: A patient never thinks that he has diarrhea: he thinks he's messing in his pants.

A patient never thinks he has encephalopathy; his head hurts! Patients reference and respond to messages that resonate with their inner thinking.

I know that the way I speak is different from you average marketing book. However this is not a Gala, it's a book wrote to wake you up.

So, if our job is to understand the patient's psychology in order to sell them our treatments as being better than those of our competition...

...we have to understand our patient's mindset – his inner thinking, his beliefs – and adapt to it.

We are not going to make our patients change their minds on anything. You can't convince people. We must adapt our messages to them.

So, again, before you spend on SEO or Google Ads, have you spent five minutes of your valuable time considering the inner thinking of somebody looking for "dentist new york"?

Who is she? How old? What is she really looking for?

I can probably assume that somebody searching for that keyword isn't necessarily a high-ticket spender.

She's either new to New York or looking for a replacement for her old dentist.

She could be looking for a dentist for her children or her grandmother; it could be anything.

The patient searching for that keyword might miss the generic knowledge of her situation, meaning they she hasn't been visited before: if she had been diagnosed parodontitis, she'd know the term and she would search for that term.

This query "Dentist New York" is a very generic one and someone who makes it might not be the best patient for you.

The competition for these generic words is tight, and they are owned by whoever has more money to acquire a customer.

If you can spend $700 to acquire a generic customer, you can still be ok with Google Ads. Yes, google ads works as an auction, the more one bids the more he gets. And yes, google ads is very expensive for these kinds of keywords.

If you'd like to have your website rank seventh or eighth (hint: You don't want this), you can try some SEO. You might find yourself spending less than with Google Ads.

As you might start to notice, you don't have to focus on the technicalities of the process. Just ask yourself a few questions:

- When will the patients see this message/ad?
- Is the message among other, similar messages in a crowd of thousands (i.e., competition) or is it unique?

- How easily can the patient get information and content about my business?
- Is this information well-presented so that I will jump out of the crowd?

These questions are the only ones that matter.

The cause-consequence thought that states *"Umh, they are looking for a dentist in New York, so if i buy 'Dentist New York' i'll get them as patients! "* is way too simplistic. Internet is made by people for people, and people's minds are a bit more complex than that.

The fact is, most landing pages (the ones that you open when you click on the "Dentist New York" ad) aren't optimized and do a poor job.

We once had a client, a dentist who specialized in advanced implantology (like many we have in our portfolio). He worked with an agency that heavily bought the "dentist" keyword on Google, related to their city. At the end of the year (a 12-month project), they had a book full of **leads**.

Leads: a sales lead is a potential sales contact, an individual that expresses an interest in your goods or services. Leads acquired by our agency are actively asking to be contacted by your front office, in order to book an appointment.

> A lead should always be called as soon as possible. Leads' temperature (their willingness to buy into your service) decreases with time.

Guess what? They were ALL shit.

Not necessarily because these people weren't interested in dental treatment but…

Having bought the generic "dentist + city" keyword..

- Most competition on Google focuses on price. By this, I mean the treatment price is a variable that is heavily shown in the ads.
- These ads were next to each other, on the same page, all asking for attention with respect to the same keyword.
- Everybody looks for more than one result before making a decision.

This is why most SEO **indexing** is about "breast augmentation price."

> **Indexing:** the process, with SEO, of having your website show-up on Google for a chosen keyword

We know that people looking for generic keywords on Google are generic patients. Sometimes they don't even know what they have. Sometimes they look out of curiosity. Somebody looking for "breast augmentation" is probably a better lead than somebody looking for "surgeon new york."

You don't want to buy that keyword.

You might be saying to yourself: Well, I have friends who made money with it. And I know and have helped people with these methods, too. But remember my grandfather? Even though he made good money building houses in 1970, that doesn't mean we will in 2019.

What worked yesterday won't necessarily work today.

Yes, people have made millions ONLY with Google ads and SEO. But now the market is pretty saturated.

Ok, I'm going to tell you what will work now for you.

It's Instagram and Facebook advertising.

Advertising on Instagram and Facebook

P.S. Facebook and Instagram share the same algorithm and are owned by the same company.

Do you spend more time on Google or Facebook? Is your ideal customer on Facebook (older ones) or Instagram (younger ones, especially good for cosmetic treatments)?

Do you know why people spend so much time on these platforms (so much that Apple introduced a software that helps you track the number of hours spent on them)?

Because these platforms are built to entertain you, but not like cable television did (for how many channels there could be, they will never be as many as the interests of people watching).

The reason why you choose the smaller screen is that you get a different set of content depending on your tastes.

Your Facebook knows you better than you know yourself.

Your Facebook listens to you when you chat on WhatsApp and when you speak on the phone or with your friends. The **algo** knows it.

Algo, or Algorithm: it's Facebook's "brain" and decides what is shown to you everyday. What is shown to you is different and unique, and is based on your behaviour on and off Facebook. Facebook tracks your behaviour and shows you content accordingly.

The algo listens to you and then comes back to people like me – people who know how to leverage the algo, people who studied the algo, who spend on the algo for you and for other clients every day.

The algo comes back to me and says, "Hey Max, this guy might be interested in what you sell."

This is probably how you got into reading this book, right? It's because the algo is my friend.

Creepy isn't it? I know. Facebook denies that the algo listens to you, but you can prove Facebook wrong. If you don't have a cat, try this.

Speak about cat food on the phone, with your phone locked. Write about it on WhatsApp. Do it now. Write to your friends about "cat food." You'd better listen to me when you find cat food ads on your Facebook news feed.

It's scary, I know, but I'll tell you something: This has helped me sell millions in treatments so far and it has helped people with severe illnesses find the right structure for them. As I told you: Nobody wants to spend one week on Google searching for a way to get his hair back (trichology). People want information now – easy information, useful information – without having to ask for it. It's the same for you, for me, for everybody. And the Facebook algo does that.

Not only can the algo make you the most important professional in your area, but it is also very likely that today, in early 2019, the algo is the ONLY way to do that.

It's such a strong tool, you'd be a fool not to use it.

How to leverage the algo

The algorithm alone is a powerful tool, the most powerful ever in selling high-ticket treatments. You can easily target people whom you never could before, and you can do it in only a few days.

These people are scrolling through their feeds in their free time, and the algo knows when to show them ads at the right moment. If somebody never purchases anything in the morning, and our budget is right, it is very unlikely that the algo will show them the ad in the morning.

I have personally used the algo to bring wealth to myself and to my clients. My clients have obtained not only wealth but also fame in their areas! That's because now, with less competition, if 100 people are looking at a single ad, one of them might be asking for an appointment now…

…while the other 99 now know about you. (Before, you were a total nobody to them.)

You see, we can't track all the conversions that the algo does. We can track around half of them. For my personal businesses, when we have, say, 200 conversions tracked in a day, I count them as 260. This is because I know that some people will see the ad and then call themselves, or order on the phone, or visit us directly. This means we can't track it all. Not all people make a decision NOW, especially for high-ticket treatments, even though our entire strategy is focused on acquiring patients in the short term.

You HAVE to use the algo on your own behalf. You need to intercept people in your country, in your area, in your city NOW who need your service. The algo knows where they are, and we know how to speak to the algo. The algo does a better job than Google does at servicing these people. And it does so at a cheaper price.

There will always be new technologies. This is why we are not specialists at Facebook or Instagram. We are specialists in only one thing: acquiring patients. Whether this is for a top-tier trichologist, or for a top hospital, that's what we do. You can use – and we use – both Google and Facebook, but now the algo is the best, cheapest, most effective way to grow your presence online and offline.

Conclusion

You don't want to use today what used to work yesterday.

You'd better be cautious because yesterday's successful techniques won't necessarily work today, even if you have a friend who achieved results.

I have personally worked with practices that spent five figures a day on Google. That budget has now moved to other, more profitable online platforms.

Back in the day, people managed to come out of nothing in crowded markets thanks to Google.

But you know what? These techniques don't work anymore.

Every ad, every platform, everything gets saturated.

You'd better act, and you'd better act fast on what works now, not what worked yesterday.

These opportunities are limited.

CHAPTER 2

Advanced strategies of targeting and retargeting

The power of the algorithm – and a case study

There's a book called *Flashboys* by Michael Lewis that talks about some guys on Wall Street who discovered a way, through technology, to get information a tiny fraction of a second before the rest of the market did. Having this leverage made them a fortune. It is a true story. It is a non-fiction book.

In the same way, the sunglasses brand "Hawkers" has been one of the first to apply a technology on Facebook that helped make a fortune for them. They did retargeting before anyone else.

What is "retargeting" and how does it apply to you as a doctor or clinic manager?

Retargeting is essentially this: When you see something you like on the internet, you click on it, you check it, you might even add it to your basket. Then, when you don't complete the purchase, you see an ad following you. It's on YouTube, it's on Instagram, it's on Facebook. It engages you. The company wants you to click again and again

And again

Until you don't buy.

Argentinian Footballer Messi is one of the Official Sponsors of the Sunglasses Brand Hawkers

The rule of seven is one of the oldest concepts in marketing. Although it is old, it isn't outdated. The rule of seven simply says that the prospective patient should hear or see a marketing message at least seven times before they accept it.

Remember when I told you to fire an agency if it doesn't use Facebook Pixel?

This is because if the company isn't using this tool, it's showing your message to your audience at most 1-2 times, burning your entire budget.

Let's say 100 people see your message about fixing their vision so that they no longer have to wear glasses.

Only 30 of them are really on target. Three of them immediately opt in and you have two visits.

You close one. You have a happy patient and a happy pocket.

We are happy too.

However, we still have 29 people on target. They wear glasses and they are not happy with them. The fact is, when the algo showed them the ad, one of the 29 was not paying attention.

Another lead was interrupted by her mother calling from the kitchen.

Another one had a ringing phone.

Some fishes need to be nurtured before you can catch them properly. Your "enemies" are not your colleagues but an holiday, a new car, lack of information, lack of attention. Lack of the driving emotions that will wake your patients up.

There are 1000 reasons why your patient might not care about you. There are 1000 moments in a day where they wouldn't notice anything in their best interest. As they wouldn't notice a 500$ bill laying on the street or the simple fact they're neglecting their health. That's why you need your message to be broadcasted more and more times to the right people.

There will be patients who immediately jump at your door. However, most will want to see you around for a while. How long is "a while"? They'll need at least one year to effectively evaluate your work.

You know the little "unsubscribe" button that every promotional mail you receive has ? Social networks like Facebook work the same except that.. They push the "unsubscribe" button for you. The reason Facebook and Instagram can be so addictive is that the algorithm shows you what you like and avoid at all cost to show you stuff you don't care.

Your communication plan for your patients and potential patients cannot contain only "marketing hooks" (e.g., marketing that invites to an instant conversion, like booking an appointment or 'shop now' etc.).

To be genuine and authentic, you must serve your patients some "marketing jabs" as content that feeds them, nurtures them, eliminates their doubts without your having to immediately ask for an appointment after that. As an health professional you should provide informative content at this stage

---

Jabs and *Hooks* are punches used in martial arts or boxing. *Jabs* are usually used as a defense punches, with your weaker arm. A *hook* is the strongest punch with your strongest arm. Usual training consists of jab, jab, jab and then hook. This process applies to marketing with Gary Vaynerchuk' book: Jab, Jab, Jab, Right Hook

The point of Vaynerchuk's thinking is that a correct marketing strategy should first feed the client with content and ask for an action only afterwards. A bit different than asking for a "Free Visit" in your clinic.

These kinds of jabs don't have to be broadcasted to the initial population of 100 people in our example above; you need only the 30. In the end, you just closed 1-3 people out of the 30, but what about the remaining 27? They're still potential patients. You can't lose them. And no, you better act as they won't remember themselves.

In everyday life, we see thousands of messages we like...and you know what? We simply forget them.

Our work is not just about acquiring patients, but about creating a brand centered on your name. Nobody should EVER forget who you are.

If your surname is Smith and you do breast augmentation, you want people to Smith-ize their breasts. This is you. You get the whole package: the status, the wealth, the respect. This must be your vision. Don't settle for less.

To do that, you need to appear on those 30 people's screens 30 times a day.

You might say that this is a bit too much. And if the patient were my mother (who definitely doesn't want a DD cup), then yes, it would be a mess.

But if the patient is somebody who has already expressed interest in you, somebody who wants those bigger breasts...guess what? The more space you invade, the more you'll become the best choice.

And another thing: You have to invade that space with fresh content. Not just the same image and the same headline for 6 months. You need to serve fresh content to the thirsty crowd. The fresher, the better.

All the competitors you secretly watch, the ones publishing content every day, are already doing this. You are at a good point reading this book, but only if you take action once you set it down.

You have to take it all; you have to be the Coca-Cola of health professionals. All your competitors, the best ones, should look like Pepsi. Your remaining competitors? Like the kind of cola you find in D-class malls. Like something of little value compared to the perception we're creating about you.

It doesn't matter if your competitors graduated with better grades or have better titles. It doesn't matter because PEOPLE DON'T CARE. If you got their attention 30 times a day, you'll notice it.

You have to be there 30 times a day with interesting content, fresh content. You have to scale, to speak to more people

When I started my first e-commerces we never found the time to invest in remarketing. We already had our sales so we thought, 'We'll care about it later.' But after growing up and getting more serious about it, we finally implemented it.

I'll tell you: Half of the sales we gain are through active follow-up and retargeting. Half of the sales we get involve either somebody who has already expressed interest in us, or somebody who has already bought our products. And this is done in an automated way. I don't have to wake up every day thinking about it to do it. Once you express interest in our products online, either you send an email, visit our shop, like one of our pictures...you immediately get into an automated flow where content is shown to you AUTOMATICALLY.

Half of your patients can be acquired with a system you actually set-up once, and then forget it.

We can track the results of these actions, and you'll see an increase from 25% to 50% of your revenue. Just by following up. In an automated way. You set up the machine and it runs itself. You just have to feed it content; the machine will automatically show the content to the hottest audience day by day.

Invest in this. Just this. Hire one fewer person. Raise your prices. Give up on equipment. Invest in this. Invest in yourself, your figure, your status, your image. Make it big.

Fame is part of the game. You can't make it big in healthcare without having a big, growing name. There's no place for modesty..

To make it, your message must be two things: simple and reiterated.

Thanks to the Facebook algo, we can reiterate your message to the people who already expressed interest in you: your fans.

Some of them aren't ready, but for a very low price, we can nurture them.

The Facebook algo likes to show people what they're into.

A panel with your face down the road costs an insane amount of money, and it speaks to everybody.

You DON'T want to deliver your message to everybody. You are not Kim Kardashian or Snookie. (P.S. Snookie wrote a book; why haven't you?) You are a professional. And a patient has, by definition, a serious problem she wants to solve NOW. You're the solution.

You'll know you're getting big when a number of people, whether colleagues or not, start attacking you. When you become a subject of controversy, you're on the right path.

But you know what? An essential skill for achieving success in any area of life is immunity to criticism.

A book is an incredible tool to create your personal brand. If Snooki from MTV's "Jersey Shore" can do it, so do you.

Video retargeting

Video Retargeting: the opportunity to re-target and re-market an audience depending on how many minutes they they watched of a video online

If you watched a one hour video on a particular kind of surgery, chances are you are very likely to be a patient on that matter. Devoting one hour of your time means you care and means you are on target with the service. This tool is one of the strongest we actually have in our arsenal.

Let's take Saverio *(Ferrari Parabita)*, one of my partners in Italy. Saverio is one of the most famous dentists in Italy and in the world. He's often invited on various TV shows to speak about advanced implantology.

When I met Saverio, I knew who I had in front of me, and I knew these TV shows were doing well. However, again, some people fall asleep in front of the TV. Other people are very interested but then they forget, or the moment isn't the right one for them to book an appointment.

Maybe there isn't a clear call to action. Or if there is, maybe the patient is reluctant to place a call at certain times of the day. (From investigating hundreds of thousands of leads, we've found that the elderly prefer phone calls in the morning.)

Another thing: TV is very expensive. You might not be Saverio; you might have high barriers to being on a TV show.

So what did we do? We didn't just advertise Saverio's TV show like it was being aired on Grandpa's mobile.

No, <u>we advertised it to the masses</u>. Then we created audiences based on the percentage of the video they watched.

Let's say you show the video to 1 million people (not the entire hour-and-a-half video, just the ad offering the opportunity to watch the video).

You'll see that:

150,000 people clicked on the ad and watched between 5 and 15 seconds of the video.

50,000 people watched 5 minutes of the video.

19,000 people watched 15 minutes of the video.

3,000 people watched over half the video.

1,190 people watched the entire video.

First, we immediately eliminated those who didn't watch enough of the video.

And the more we tightened up the audience, the better our results.

Video retargeting gave us the power to show the message many times to the people who showed the most interest. The result was massive.

Those 1,190 people who watched over an hour and a half of your content...well, you should have a clue as to how nurtured they are.

How interested they are in the subject matter.

How hot this audience is, how into you they are BEFORE they even get to your door.

I'm disclosing my strategies here, knowing that half of the readers of this book are in the health word. The other half are in the marketing world, trying to get some tricks they can use with their clients.

But I don't care because we're always researching new trends and techniques. What worked yesterday might not work today.

> Though this be madness, yet there is method in 't.
> *Hamlet - Act 2, Scene 2*

At this point in the book, you should start to understand what we do and the logic behind it.

If you know the logic, you rationally understand why somebody who watched a video about you for an hour and a half is a better lead than somebody who looks for "dentist new york".

I hope you get it. If you didn't before reading this book, you're forgiven. If you don't now, you're committing an unforgivable sin.

If your agency isn't retargeting your marketing messages, fire it. That agency is wasting your money. Retargeting gets you the cheapest traffic. That's because it involves showing content to somebody who already loves your content. Facebook is still what it is because it really cares about getting you hooked on the platform. It doesn't show you which advertiser paid the most to show you an ad; rather, it shows you what you want to see.

Facebook's bidding system doesn't work simply according to "whoever pays more gets more attention."

If somebody tries to advertise something that Facebook or its users (you) don't want to see, you can put as much money out there as you want, but Facebook will show less and less of your advertisement.

Facebook understands what its users (you) like or don't like based on whether they click or don't click, the amount of time they stay away from Facebook, whether you purchase something or send an email, etc.

All this information is tracked. We have it in our computers, too.

Feed your retargeting audience with fresh content every week, and you will find yourself gaining a good number of fans. These are the people who talk about you even if they haven't personally met you. They think you're the best even though you haven't treated them. They do this not because somebody told them about you but because you feed them content week after week, enough so that you're taking up space inside their minds.

That space, that perception, is the most valuable thing you have. More than your degree. More than your house. More than anything.

You are going to be referred to as a "celebrity" or an "expert" by people who never visited your practice or tried your services. This is the power of showing the right message to the right audience.

The stronger the video's emotional resonance, the better the results. People choose with their bellies, their hearts (and sometimes, other parts of the body) but NEVER with their brains.

This applies to you, too. I could show you our results in a boring way—real, tangible results—and you couldn't care less. You need entertainment, right?

As a health professional, you don't have to act like I do. However, you have to make your prospective clients fall in love with you.

Because anxiety is the most common trait in a patient seeking treatment, I usually advise clients to communicate relaxation and self-awareness in their content—without being boring.

However strong your message is, if you show it to your audience only once or twice, you'd be better served spending time with the kids.

Remember how often Obama spoke about change? Whether or not you like him, you have to admit that you heard the word "change" 30 times a day, for months.

Obama got elected.

Do you remember McCain's message? I don't. Do you remember Hillary's message? What was it, by the way? Whether you love it or hate it, everybody knows about "the wall."

What I'm telling you is that the algo gives you the power to speak to only your biggest fans in an effective, efficient way. You don't have to speak to an entire country.

Any marketing plan that doesn't have a clear remarketing strategy isn't regarding viewers as patients or people BUT rather as numbers. They're not numbers.

When we're writing ads, it's like we're writing a letter to my mum. You're speaking to your mum, your uncle, your best friend. Don't speak like a TV commercial. Stay relaxed. Don't use the language you learned at school.

Your patients' thoughts are easy, simple, dualistic. Pain/No Pain. Expensive/not expensive. And they will quickly forget your message if you don't repeat it at least 100 times.

A patient acquisition campaign is a good investment in your practice. But here we're talking about something more. A single 1-month campaign can't change your life. Obama didn't speak about change for a month and then stop.

Not just retargeting: Targeting

You can target people on Facebook based on what they like, their behavior, their age. You can do this based not only on what they do on the platform but also, surprisingly, what they do off it.

I'm not talking about the basic targeting offered by the infamous "boost post" button on your Facebook page. When you combine various software programs and get access to Facebook Business Manager, the possibilities are nearly endless.

That "boost post" button is for making a quick buck. Not for you, but for them: Facebook Company. I don't care if one day you spent $20 on a Facebook post and got 12 likes. This is not what we're talking about and you're not a Facebook marketer. "Boosting posts" is not Facebook marketing.

I roll my eyes when clients talk about their secretaries or "social media managers" boosting posts. This isn't what we're talking about in this book.

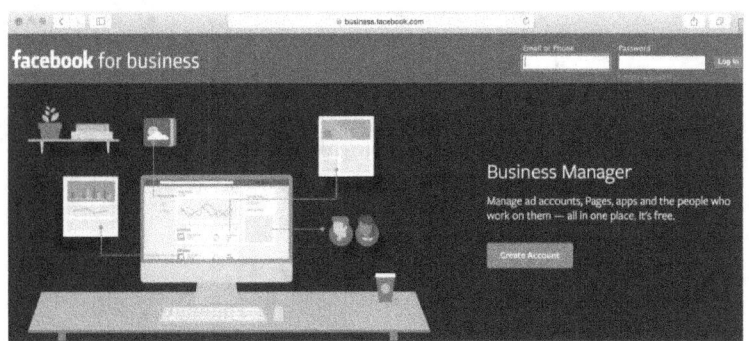

All effective online marketing starts from here. You won't be profitable boosting posts directly from your Facebook page

We can target certain demographics, certain ethnicities, people who are into Oprah.

And there comes the game. I bet that somebody 65-70 years old who takes dance classes would be VERY interested in dental implants.

Boom.

And somebody 70+ with an interest in political news might be a good pick for hearing aids.

Most of my best leads aren't targeted as "dentists" but individuals interested in CAD/CAM dentistry.

We can target it down to your favorite shoe brand, your favorite TV show, your income.

Facebook watches you on and OFF the platform. When you're on any website with a Facebook pixel installed on it, Facebook is watching you. It can recognize your IP even when you're not logged into Facebook.

When you click, from Facebook, into any website, Facebook sees how long you're going to be there; it can gauge your level of interest in the subject.

The algo knows you better than you know yourself. I hope you're less on the creepy side and more on the "I can use this to my advantage" side.

On the other hand, I can assure you that nobody is personally watching your inbox or spying on you from Facebook. Because nobody cares.

The data has value only once it is big data. With big data, we can influence the masses and impose our roles as the first in our category.

In the end, when somebody thinks about "bariatric surgery," they are going to think about YOU and only you. You don't have enough paper or ink to fill your city with billboards about you. However, we can fill the web with videos and photos and content about you. It's going to be cheaper.

As with anything, the first who arrives in the mind is the leader of any category. If you want to be the Coke of colas or the Starbucks of coffee, you have to act fast and be persistent. This game starts as a strategy for acquiring patients, bringing you insane rewards, but it then must become a wider brand strategy regarding your role as a professional in your area.

Whoever shows up first takes it all.

CHAPTER 3

How to generate and acquire high-ticket patients on an industrial scale

Rules of the game and the importance of content

You might have been fooled into thinking that the internet is a unique place. Maybe you enjoy using your personal Facebook or Instagram but have been told that most of the internet plays by different rules.

I'll tell you something that you'd better remember: The internet is a channel, just like any other.

Marketing on the internet is no different from marketing on billboards or TV. What changes is the psychology of the person reading the messages (which itself is affected by the device that the person is using and by the moment when that person sees your message). The tools are also different.

With the internet, we have more tools. We can track, measure, and scale at a deeper level, faster and with a stronger impact.

With the internet, people can take action immediately and more easily.

Cars are now driving themselves and soon you'll be able to buy things in the blink of an eye. You can already do this with home services through Alexa. Do you think all this won't affect your job? The fact that the seniors in this game had easier rules to follow doesn't mean that you will.

The game is changing and so are the rules.

Once upon a time, in the 60s and 70s, if you were a big company, you broadcast an ad on TV. If the client saw an increase in upfront revenue, the ad was working. The agency would be hired again.

Obviously, this is a very stupid way to work, but you never have the tools you want. If you have any kind of sales, you know that they're not constant. They change. You can't measure a marketing campaign based on top-line revenue. You can't just say, "Hey, if we see a top revenue increase, it means the campaign is working!"

Measuring is always needed. You need it as a tool to do a better job.

You make it, you adjust it, you fix it: boom.

Making it and then *hoping* top-line revenue will increase is not the way we work. Your top line might decrease for 1,000 reasons you don't know about. You want to be in control of what we're delivering to you. Believing that something will increase is not being in control. Without control, you can't drive a car, a plane, a boat, or a company. You need complete control over your marketing decisions.

To acquire patients on a larger scale, we have to do one thing you have probably never done: Measure every campaign to the needle. I don't work with clients who don't measure, and a red flag lights up my eyes when I notice that all previous marketing efforts haven't been measured.

This means you're marketing because "you have to" when you should be marketing because you love it. You don't start an online campaign because everyone else is doing it. You start it because it will be an active part of your overall marketing strategy – a strategy aimed at taking all you can, starting with all you've got.

So, to acquire patients on an industrial scale, you must commit to measuring every cent spent on marketing, doing the best, in conjunction with offline methods, to measure it.

You can measure offline using different phone numbers for calls to action or promotions, etc.

Content

Now let's dive deep into what patients are really looking for, and what we have to provide them on an industrial scale so that they will accept our quote.

1. They want to be informed.
2. They want a valid, emotional reason to choose.

Nothing more. And I know you spent millions of dollars over the years on things that don't relate to what I'm talking about.

How much of your budget is spent on informing the patient? How much of your budget is spent on giving them a valid, emotional reason to choose you and not your competitor down the street?

Be honest.

You got sold on machines, masters, university, staff, equipment.

But just two things bring people to your door. This is what I say to my team every time we have a new hire in the copy department. I say, "Guys, patients need to be informed and they need a strong, emotional reason to choose our client. Let's get back to work and show me what you can do."

And here the magic happens.

Now let me take you by the hand and show you these focal points in detail.

They want to be informed.

This is what your grandfather's doctor used to do in the silence of his study, surrounded by hills and cottages, in the good old authority of a typical countryside doctor.

Those days are gone. Information is free. Your patient, at every level of instruction or income, will search for her problem on the internet; the one who provides the best information wins.

Once upon a time, nobody could speak a word when the good old doctor spoke. If one day the doctor told all the peasants to walk barefoot, they would. If he urged the countryside to eat bananas, they'd eat bananas.

Unfortunately for you, those days are gone. You already have patients whom the internet has poorly informed. Patients who reply to what you prescribe them. It's because of the internet, you know. Now they think they know it all. They want to know everything. Even though you might have been working for 20-30 years, they still want to know more than you do.

These patients received unclear information about their situation. They are confused. You are going to win them the day you take the time to explain, carefully, step by step, the situation they are facing, what you are going to do, and how much they are going to pay.

I'm confident most of you can do this in the quiet of your study, where empathy is created between you and the patient.

However, to acquire patients on a large scale, you'll have to broadcast that empathy on a large scale. And here we go.

You'll need videos to broadcast to your patients/fan base and you'll have to broadcast those videos at least weekly.

You'll have to cover every point of the process; it is going to be a huge, time-consuming task for you.

However, instead of speaking to one patient at a time, you will have the leverage to speak to 10, 100, or 1,000 patients at a time. The consequence is going to be mind-blowing for you.

And again, I will tell you something that will make you instant money.
Please don't talk about how good you are, how "quality" is important to you and your team, how much you care, how big and nice your rooms or your products are.

Because nobody actually cares.

Speak about their problem, their pain. You want to describe the pain so well that they say, "Hey, that is my pain exactly."

And you won't describe the pain as you learned it in school. School is over. Here, we are in real life. You don't use a language that a 6-year-old would not understand. You speak to them as if they were babies.

Reserve bombastic language for your colleagues. Start explaining the pain as if you know every little facet, all the aggravation they might be feeling.

When speaking to obese patients, describe the legs touching each other when walking, the rubbing. The embarrassment, the tiredness. Keep a detached attitude but be direct.

And again: These are not cheeseburgers. I don't care how McDonald's makes cheeseburgers. If I'm getting a $250 treatment, I want to know EVERYTHING. And I'm saying $250. Not $25,000. Not even $2,500. If I am going to go through a $250 treatment (let's say frenuloplasty), I want to know EVERYTHING about it before getting the surgery. And it's not because I attended university. Anybody would do this in the age of the internet.

What caused my pain, how long it could last if I don't treat it, the risks, the consequences, how to prepare for the treatment, how to avoid surprises, what I will get by paying the premium you charge as opposed to going with your competitors.

Back on track: We agreed that your patient wants to be informed, at the deepest level possible.

We agreed that this communication can't happen one-on-one in your study, like in the good old days.

And we agreed that this communication must be broadcast. It must be simple, easy to say, easy to listen to, something that sticks in the mind.

Now: No, your website isn't what I'm talking about. In 99% of cases (I'd actually say 100%), your website is full of stuff nobody is interested in, written in a language that is too difficult to understand, with content that is distributed, in the best scenario, throughout categories and subcategories.

And no, nobody is on your website now. Even if you're grossing $6 million a year, the only reason somebody visits your $25,000 website is to find your address.

Inside yourself, you know that what I'm saying is right. Spending thousands on website-building makes no sense if you don't advertise. You don't buy Gucci or Louboutin and just stay home. Don't ever spend on a website; spend on patient attraction. Spend on patient retention. Invest in patient acquisition!

This is not building your website from scratch. Leave that to your SEO agency. We do not have time; we have to start acquiring patients NOW. Investing in online patient acquisition is not website-building.

We build a funnel instead. What is a funnel? Simply put, it's a simpler website made from scratch by us, for you. This website contains several pages in sequence. You don't decide where to go; you can go in only one direction. And we decide that direction. We decide what content you will see, in sequence. And guess what? We decide the sequence, too.

The first steps of the funnel will be made for the masses. The more a patient goes through a funnel, the more that patient is a good fit for us, for your clinic, your practice, your hospital. For your product.

Essentially, the funnel continues in your practice. When a patient speaks with you, after you have visited with him, after he has paid for the first visit – these are all steps in the funnel. If you had to compare an online funnel to an average website, the main differences would be:

- In a funnel, several buttons bring all visitors to the same destination (the next step of the funnel). On a website, you have different sections and you assume that people spend the weekend surfing them.
- Because a funnel has fewer steps, you have more control and can tweak what doesn't work. With traffic divided into steps, it will be easier to understand when people get stuck and, thus, to work only on that part of the funnel.

The job is to bring the best leads in the largest numbers to your door. Your job is to call/answer them, visit with them, have them accept the treatment quote. Your job is to do the best job, greet them, ask them for referrals, and have them come back again and again (if needed).

The clients we work with best already have:

- A script for how the front desk will call and assess leads.
- A script for how the assistant will introduce the doctor to the patient (or the product to the patient).
- A script for how the doctor will quote the treatment to the patient.

We assume you already have written, registered protocols for managing leads, prospects, and patients. You can't acquire patients on a huge scale without them.

All protocoled, all systemized, all measured. All done before we work on acquiring patients. If you already have the horse, I know how to make it run pretty fast. If you're on a donkey, I can still give it a few kicks, but that's not our job

Lead generation can't save a struggling business. It can double the revenue of a good business that was not taking advantage of the opportunity. However, it's not like playing bingo at the casino. We acquire patients on an industrial scale. "Industrial" should trigger, in your head, the labour and capital-intensive part. It should trigger the automated processes, from assistant to assistant, shared among the whole team. And the massive results.

In conclusion

So: First, even before speaking about why they should choose you, before everything, we make sure we inform our patients about you in the best, most simple way. You already know the questions they ask you time and again. Record 100 patients and you will find that the same questions recur again and again.

Make sure this information is easily available, repeated, and illustrated from different angles and fresh, new perspectives.

Then...

We give them a valid, emotional reason to choose us.

This is one of the most important parts of the book. This part alone is worth a million dollars for those who take advantage of it online.

The reason must be valid, must be EMOTIONAL, and must present us as the natural best choice.

Think about what you've just read and compare it to yourself. If I asked you why a patient would choose you (which is a question I've posed to hundreds of professionals, hundreds of time), how much would you bet that I know the answer?

It's just you and me. I'm asking you, "Hey, why should patients choose you?"

Close your eyes and think about it, then come back here.

Done?

Ok, now, if you thought somebody should choose you for the high quality of your services, go and wash your face with cold water.

I have seen hundreds of people, including surgeons and marketing managers. We're sitting at a table and I ask them, "Why should any patient choose you?"

They all answer, "For *blah, blah, blah*, QUALITY."

Quality is not a skill you have or an asset of your company/practice/personal branding. There is no quality on earth, and not because it is subjective (it is). Rather, it's because quality is something that is given as granted, always.

Everyone in the world has this except sanitary professionals. Why choose me? Because of the "quality" I bring to the table.

I haven't met a sanitary professional – a doctor, surgeon, dentist, hospital manager, hearing aid managing director – who doesn't quote QUALITY as their selling point.

If I go on your website or Facebook page and I find, even once, the word "quality" used to refer to yourself, you owe me $1,000, ok? Play this game with your colleagues.

Rick and Morty Quote of the Day
@RickMortyQOTD

Segui

What?! Every hospital claims to have the best doctor in the ga-a-a-alaxy! It's like those pizza places that claim to have the best pizza in the world. W-w-what do you think they have pizza contests?! Have you ever been to a pizza contest?!
#RickandMorty #picklerick @RickandMorty

People don't choose with their wallets or brains. Even in the most important, desperate situations in their lives, they choose with emotions. They later justify with logic what was once moved by emotions. And when I say "patient" I don't mean "them" as an indistinct group of people. I mean us.

Your patient is not an analytical bean counter who will balance all the pros and cons and then judge and act.

What emotional impact does the word "quality" or the words "free visit" have on your communication? You might still get the patient through the door; if you're lucky, some other talented marketer of the "quality & free visit" legion hasn't passed through there yet. The patient might still accept the quote, but that will not be dependent on or nurtured by the campaign.

Because if all you can communicate emotionally is that you have quality and that the first visit is free, well … you are not doing marketing. You're just promoting some stuff.

You're not building a brand, you're not nurturing leads. Better than nothing, worse than most.

Let's consider an example to make it clear: hearing aids.

Target Patients: The elderly
Benefit: Being able to hear again
Solution: Your product

Now let's pretend we are bringing this product to the market

Stating that you have a quality product will not make an impact. Why choose your hearing aids? *"Because they are quality hearing aids"*

That would sound good if we were living in 1820 (maybe).

Stating that the first visit is free might bring people to the door, for sure. But generic offers equal generic leads. Someone who comes in for a free visit is not necessarily the best patient for you. You might find some gold in the pile, but that's not the best way to do the job.

Too many free visits might place pressure on your structure, especially in a crowded and saturated market.

However, there are what I call leverages, emotional leverages, that can turn your company upside down.

If you research, as we did, you might think that most elderly people would like to hear again, *so that they can listen to the birds singing.*

Lovely, isn't it? Unfortunately, my research raises the point that the ability to hear birds sing, while poetic, won't give these patients the necessary drive to pay for a $7,000 treatment.

But you know what does? Being scared that your sons will take you to a retirement home as they see you age, as they see you not hearing what they say when they speak to you.

You know what drives emotions? The story of an elderly woman who can't babysit her nephew because the parents are afraid that she does not have the independence to do it.

So, our hearing aids are no longer "quality" hearing tools, but tools that, within the story, give independence back to a woman – a strong woman.

You get what I mean when I say that we can turn your brand, your product, your hospital upside down? It's not "the internet." The internet is a tool. It's the message, the content. The emotions we provoke after all informative questions have been answered.

The internet is the best tool, today, to promote stories. You can be on everyone's mobile phone, and you can be there with a story that elicits an immediate response from the patient, whether it's a phone call, a completed information form, or the booking of an appointment.

It's about the story. The story you're talking about. Can your audience relate to your story? Is your story reliable, real, backed by real-life testimonials? Is your story buried on a 25-page funnel or it is readily accessible, propagated, filmed, broadcast to the thousands of elderly people in your area?

When I say "content" I don't mean pictures of your dentist chairs. I mean this: your story, their story. A story to which your patient can relate.

When I say "story" I mean that you should, before reading this book, document every patient's journey. Their fears, their hopes. The treatment. And how they are afterward. Produce this kind of content now, distribute it on a large, industrial scale, and see your status as a professional, your wealth, reach new, unimaginable heights.

In conclusion, I want to make it clear for you. You first have to document and inform, and to do so in the best, simplest way. You do it with authority while using simple language. You are speaking to 5-year-old children now. You're a professor.

Then you take this informative content and propagate it on the largest scale. The greater the number of people who see it, the better. People can't see it only 1-2 times. This stuff has to remain stuck in their heads. You have to be persistent day after day; you can't play this game for 6 months and then give up.

You play the game all life long. Starting today.

You catch the online ball now because it's hot now, today, and you don't know what other balls, if any, will be there tomorrow.

Then, after they are informed, they are calm, they know it's right to go on, they need a valid, emotional reason to choose you and only you. Otherwise, you will have persuaded them to obtain the treatment – but they might pursue it with somebody else.

And you don't want to work for somebody else.

Now it's time to tell a story. Beforehand, you might want to ask your patients questions that differ from the usual, diagnostic questions you ask.

These questions must dive deep into your patients' emotions. These are the questions they might not be happy to hear. The strongest leverage is often the most intimate one.

Once you have the leverage, we need a story, and the story must tie you to the patient.

Finally: The story cannot be told by you personally, the authority on the matter. Rather, it must be told by someone who has lived it. It has to be a real story. Every day you have stories going on your desk. But you saw patients, you saw "quality" and "free visits." Numbers.

There is so much more, especially for high-ticket treatments. So many tears, such strong emotions. Lives completely changed in one day.

Once you have all this, you must package and broadcast it on the largest scale. Today I gave you the blueprint to change the way you see your profession, your product, your hospital.

In other circumstances, I see competitors selling "quality" or "free visits."

But you give sight to the blind, you give teeth to the toothless. What you do has the strongest impact on your patient's life. Think of an iPhone; what does it really do better than any other mobile? It's just a mobile. You probably do something that has a bigger – 1,000 times bigger – impact on someone's life. It's time to communicate this the right way.

Don't think numbers, think stories.

CHAPTER 4

Ask your agency these questions (or any agency prospecting you)

How to stop wasting money on marketing

You probably haven't had the best experience with agencies. Most agencies are accused of not caring enough about their clients or of being focused on selling useless services (we're going to make you a new logo, a new website, etc.) on their own behalf.

Once you reach a certain size, you might outsource most of your marketing to agencies, not because they're really good at it and not because you're doing a good job of tracking what they're doing but because you don't know anything about the matter and your conscience is clear when you hire somebody else to take care of it.

Most agencies don't have a lean structure. This means that when they have to pay the utility bills … well, it's time to create new logos again.

But actually, if you don't have clear positioning, a strategy, a clear daily/weekly content flow about you and your practice, you don't need a logo. A logo won't help.

And, yes, most agencies – even the biggest ones – aren't profitable. You don't want to have a broke agency take care of your marketing.

Another error most agencies make is having many different customers. Don't blame your agency for not doing a good job if all its clients are plumbers, pizzerias, architects, and so on. Yes, marketing is the same and applies to everyone the same way, but the processes for getting results on a large scale are optimized if you work on a specific niche.

What I'm saying is: You need a specialist. A specialist will better understand your needs.

That's why we work with patients. Every time the word "patient" appears, we are there. We don't do plumbers. We don't do restaurants. We don't do real estate. We acquire patients, whether it is for a treatment that restores one's sight or a treatment that generates a head full of hair.

I wrote this chapter thinking about somebody who might not be able to afford our service but who still needs marketing assistance. You probably need this. I'll help you understand how to choose the right agency for you.

1. If it does online, do this.

Why did I write "if" it does online? Because most agencies still don't do online. I mean, posting pictures on Facebook of you and your colleagues drinking coffee is not "online." Spending thousands on paid traffic every month is doing online.

Now, a quick check to determine whether your agency knows what it's doing.

Open your PC and, using Chrome, download the 'Facebook Pixel Helper extension'.

Got it? Now visit your prospecting agency's website or landing page. Once there, check (by clicking on the extension on the top right side of your navigation bar) whether the website has Facebook Pixel.

Facebook Pixel Helper
Learn More

No pixels found on www.cnbc.com

Yep, 2 billions people on Facebook and yet Cnbc isn't optimized for it. They are wasting millions of dollars everyday because of this

Facebook Pixel Helper
Learn More

2 pixels found on www.economist.com

Facebook Pixel   View Analytics
Pixel ID: 570990896342688

▶ 🔺 PageView

▶ 🔺 ViewContent

▶ ⚡ Button Click Automatically Detected

▶ ⚡ Microdata Automatically Detected

▶ ⚙ Lytics Audiences

Facebook Pixel   View Analytics
Pixel ID: 1800435846942578

▶ ⚙ PageView

Seems like "The Economist" is well equipped and can both retarget its readers and optimize its Facebook Ads

If you get "no pixel found on yourblablaagency.com," I suggest you ask your agency why no pixels are installed.

The answer will be, *"Uh, um, mmm, why are you asking that?"*

At that point, you say that Facebook Pixel is essential for both optimizing Facebook campaigns and creating a retargeting or lookalike audience for your traffic.

Without using a Facebook pixel any dollar spent on Facebook is useless. You need it both to run your Facebook campaigns and show your content to whoever has expressed interest in it!

A Facebook pixel is a code you install on your website/landing page. It "reads" and intercepts your website visitors behaviour

Later, I will explain in detail what I'm talking about here. If your agency does not have Pixel in 2019, it means a few things:

- It's using outdated methods.
- It relies only on its "name," which can be a very bad thing for your wallet.

- It isn't building a list of prospects who visit its landing page (which is very stupid; you shouldn't do it with your patients).
- If it advertises itself using ads, the ads are not optimized (the agency doesn't know how to use the algo).

Essentially, you need this code installed on every website you advertise. If your agency says it is good at Facebook marketing but it doesn't have Pixel installed, the agency is driving a car without knowing how to turn the steering wheel.

2. It tells you that you're "first page" on something but you see no sales as a result of it.

This is the most common agency scam. An agency prospects you and promises that you will be first page on any given keyword. You find out that you are first page on that keyword because from every website you visit, you see your name appearing first. However, you get no sales. How is this possible?

It's easy; the agency did the work on a keyword that has no searches. Nobody searches for that keyword, so whether you're first or last, nobody cares.

The agency probably did not rank you for "Snail races Bangladesh 2016" but I need to tell you something: If you live in a tiny area, most combinations like "Your name; tiny area" probably gets very few searches every month.

Essentially, this means you paid for something that is not useful. Always make sure you're paying for the right keywords. "Dentist new york" is probably too expensive, but even if "your name;dentist;tiny town" is cheap, it might not be worth buying because there are not enough searches for it.

3. It asks for only a little money.

Believe it or not, you can be a pig in your job but what will bring you patients is marketing. Marketing is your name, and nothing matters more. You want to invest 1,000 USD a month in your name? You get what you pay for. You want the fame, the wealth, the status of being the best in your field? You'll have to test different agencies, different budgets, different strategies. You'll have to study marketing so that when you speak with me, you'll know what we're talking about. You have to be smart.

Anyone in India or Bangladesh can make a website for very little money. A website is meaningless in most cases. What matters more is the skill that brings patients to you. Stop. Don't care about likes, followers, websites: bullshit. Who is bringing patients to doctors or to hospital doors? If your agency isn't, fire it.

Don't trust agencies that ask for little money. This means they are not serious or structured (or, in the best cases, you're taking advantage of them). You are NOT grocery shopping. Just as you despise patients asking for "discounts" or complaining about why they got a diagnosis for $150, and you despise your colleagues selling their services for way less than you do (knowing that they're selling something worth little), be AWARE that bringing patients to your door is not a different skill in terms of price and results. You don't want to save on this. You definitely want to have a good return on investment but you want a structure that dives DEEP into it. The leads you won't acquire because you're on a tight budget will soon be someone else's leads.

And take care; this is not information you can find easily online. If your competitors are doing an extra 100,000 a month thanks to online, they will not notify you about that. When dental chains made millions thanks to Google AdWords, they did not release this publicly because they don't want you to know.

Most of our clients (unless we don't agree with them before) don't want their competitors to know they're working with us and that they're profitable. Guess why?

4. It has never worked with patient acquisition strategies.

The psychology behind buying a cheeseburger is a bit different from having your back finally free of pain or losing 40 kilograms through a surgical treatment. Low-ticket product sales are different from choosing an expensive procedure that can save/restore your life.

One of my clients told us that, after reading our sales pages, customers were selling their cars to afford treatments. While this didn't surprise us, it should make you think. Are the ads that you're currently running making people want to sell their cars in order to receive your treatments? If not, it's probable that your services are being advertised as if they were cheeseburgers. They're not.

Think with me: Do you want a cheeseburger? There are at least two or three times during the day when you would answer "yes."

Do you want a full-arch implantology treatment for $15,000? How many times a day do you fancy that?

I see thousands of ads like this. General ads, stupid ads. Ads that don't make a sale. Ads that acquire zero patients. Ads that cost thousands of dollars, paid by inexperienced professionals to incompetent agencies. You don't want that kind of ad, do you?

5. It is very "nice."

I am guilty of not being the nicest person in the room, of firing clients, of not caring whether you're worth hundreds of thousands or millions. However, I have results. The results and knowledge that you will see in this book are real. They're the reason why I don't have to be fake-nice to you. I don't need your money. If you have a budget, run away from "nice people." They're nice for the budget, not for you. I'm not in the business of kissing up to someone because they own a hospital or pharmacy. We create results and get paid for that.

Somebody who can double your business WILL NOT be an easily available, excessively nice person.

6. It has no face.

As soon as you bring real results to the people you work with, and as soon as you have them writing daily about how happy they are to your mobile and your assistants, you'll want to stand apart from the crowd. You'll want everyone to know it. You can't last years without that.

I put my face into everything I do (except for some bikini businesses – for obvious reasons, they don't suit me well) and I'm really proud of what we're building every day.

When someone jumps on our wagon (i.e. gets hired by our company), I speak with them about their values and their goals and determine whether they align with those of our agency. I can interview an intern for five hours straight, as nothing matters more than the people we hire.

Ask the agency about its results in terms of patient acquisition. Ask to speak to its clients. If the agency tries to avoid this, fire it. In the early days, we worked for free to get a portfolio of clients. So should they if they want to work in this tough game that is patient acquisition.

7. It isn't sharp.

I want to tell you something: I'm tired of seeing agencies and "marketing professionals" wearing vests and silly hats, doing stupid stuff in the office, like "in this office, we have fun."

I'll tell you a secret: In my office, there is no fun. We work. Fun is for outside the office.

In our offices, I want people to look sharp and clean. I know that Mark Zuckerberg wears t-shirts but most people working in marketing ARE NOT Mark Zuckerberg and won't make a fraction of what he does. So you should dress sharp and look sharp. On this point, I see most sanitary professionals doing things right.

8. It is not a company.

I suggest that you hire somebody from India on Fiverr if you need work like basic video editing, managing an Instagram account post sequence, or simple graphics. Getting patients to your door isn't the same thing as drawing a logo. A logo won't bring patients to your door.

I don't care about logos, and you don't care about them either. Coca-Cola is not famous because of its logo. Don't waste money on stupid stuff. The only asset you have is your relationship with your patients and your ability to bring MORE of them to your door.

So, again: You don't hire a "freelancer" or somebody who just graduated in marketing studies to take care of your online/physical communication. No group of "young guys" will get you business simply by clicking on a MacBook. Grow up and accept your responsibilities. Study marketing and get the skills to understand who can help you and who cannot.

Some professionals (hopefully not you) believe this story: I have a business; now these guys will click on the computer and we'll get tons of sales!

My colleagues in web development, at every level, are getting asked by serious business people to make websites "like Facebook."

"Hey, I have a $25,000 budget. Can we make a website like Facebook, but for lawyers?"

This is real stuff and it is happening every day. Please study an argument before paying $1 for it.

A freelancer can help you with a few things, but whatever they sell you, they won't be able to do much more. They won't transform your business. You should know this yourself, without me writing about it.

The only person who cares about bringing patients to the door is you. That is why you don't see your assistant's assistant reading books like this. They couldn't care less. It is your responsibility to act now on new opportunities to bring more patients to your door.

However, every hospital has a guy who "manages social" and gets paid $30,000 a year, fresh out of college, for clicking on his computer. He has a nice Instagram account … why not give him the passwords?

Most hospitals are paying $30,000 a year to give some Millennials their Facebook and Instagram passwords. Count the hours and count the money flowing out.

All this is happening now.

9. It is a "creative."

When it comes to bringing patients to your door, I'm not a creative. It's not about how nice your website looks (the color, the touch, etc.). It's not about how "crazy" we are with our sweet oddness that makes us special and unique.

Again, it's about bringing the right patients – the high-ticket ones – to the right door: yours. We are not looking to be provocative, funny, interesting, or colorful.

Especially in sanitary, there is no relationship between how creative your ads are and how effective they are … and you buy ads for their effectiveness. If you buy something purely for its beauty, I'm glad you have good taste but that's something worth hanging on your home's walls, not something worth promoting.

10. It has too many bills.

Just as most of your patients' decision patterns are faulty, so too are your own decision patterns wrong when you choose an agency.

As human beings, we score too low on objectivity. We should go only for proven results. Most of you are easily charmed by big offices with large staffs.

Now I'll tell you something: An agency's revenue is not correlated with the results it creates for its clients.

It's the same concept as a surgeon's success not being related to his or her handiwork.

You know this story already; maybe some of your worst classmates are making a good living now regardless of their lack of medical expertise.

However, when you visit a doctor, you don't want the one who's making the most money.

Likewise, when you hire an agency, you don't want the one with the biggest office and the biggest name.

Don't be fooled by the assistant's looks; ask for results, always. They are more important than anything else.

Ask this question: Have you ever acquired patients online? If yes, when? With what results? Can I speak to one of your clients?

11. It has lots of enthusiasm.

If the agency has lots of enthusiasm right away, that's not a good sign. It reminds me of people who don't know how to do business. You don't do business with enthusiasm, which will fade away.

You do business with facts. The more facts the agency asks you, the more it probably cares, and the more it cares, the better for you. This applies at any level. An account executive must care, and so must anyone behind you.

I'll tell you something: Our clients' secretaries or front office staff HATE US. We come from one day to another and we fill their agendas with patients to call. The number of patients can be huge. The front office staff has to call them all, and if the patients don't answer, we have a system that checks on whether your staff called them a second or third time. Your staff prefers to watch Instagram on their mobiles than to make 20+ calls a day. These calls can last 30 minutes each. Not all calls will result in visits, and that can be frustrating. You'd better prepare your staff before you work with us, as we're going to overload them.

Knowing that we'll probably put pressure on a client's infrastructure, I never enthusiastically accept a new client. I try to be realistic; I don't want to tell the client what the client wants to hear.

The client wants me to tell her that with some mouse clicks I will make her rich while she lays on the couch.

That's not what we do. Lead Gen can't save a struggling business, especially one with a poor infrastructure. It works best when it is a wheel in a marketing strategy. It works in concert with offline, with how you greet your patients and what services you're selling.

It works in terms of how you differentiate yourself from your competition. It works. It is making millions of dollars for our clients today. Now. But it is not easy money. It won't differ from the hard-earned money you have already made.

If the agency sells you dreams, run.

12. Advanced: It doesn't restore the old campaigns.

I'll tell you something you don't know. Campaigns, even the most successful ones, die.

There's something I've seen with a few people who manage to do work similar to ours: When a campaign dies, they keep it going for however long the agreement lasts.

Obviously, if you have 100 different clients in 100 different niches, it will be much more difficult for your agency to rearrange a new online campaign for each one.

If you plan to stick with an agency for the long term, you should ensure that the campaigns change if they stop producing the desired results.

Again: Owning a practice is not like owning an e-commerce. You don't do all your business online and you don't spend all your marketing budget online. Your business has hidden opportunities you probably don't know (either in referral strategies or follow-up strategies).

You spend your budget on online advertising as long as you're profitable. As patients' money often comes immediately, you have the leverage to 10X your investment. If something works with a $3,000-$4,000 monthly investment and you're highly profitable, you should press the pedal. Either somebody else is acquiring those patients or you are. You should press the pedal for as long as your structure can sustain it.

13. It says yes to everything.

I see this all the time. You ask the agency: Can you take care of my YouTube? Can you do this on my website? Can you manage my email list? And the agency immediately says: Yes. This isn't good.

You are probably reading this because you have become good at doing only one thing, whether you're the best in rhinoplasty or you're a hospital manager.

We don't take care of your YouTube page and upload your video when you want. We simply don't do that – especially if you ask for it without an underlying problem. If you're badly staffed, we can help you find a good social media manager to hire. However, we don't do little tasks and you should beware of anyone who always says "yes" to them.

We do one thing and we're the best at it. We're not generalists and we don't do everything online. We specialize in bringing patients to your door. To do that on the necessary scale, we need to be focused.

So should you. If you have a treatment and you think you differ from your competition, and if that treatment is a high-ticket sell, we know how to sell it. Whether you can implant teeth in a mouth that has little bone or implant hair on a head at a competitive cost, we're in business and you can gross six figures with our services. We know how to reach your patients, the same way we reached you.

14. Again: It offers you SEO services.

Wouldn't it be wonderful if, by traveling through time, we were able to bring fire to the prehistoric era? What huge advantage would the Romans have if we could bring fire-weapons to them in 100 A.C.

However, imagine visiting President Kennedy and showing him how you could re-shape the US economy with the invention of print.

What was successful in the past cannot be used today. Never. An enormous amount of wealth was gained by savvy sanitary professionals who leveraged SEO at the beginning.

But not now. Anybody offering you SEO services in 2019 for a keyword like " dentist new york" is just trying to take your money.

I want to be straight with you: I like money too, but Mother Nature gave me the arrogance to believe I can exchange it for something valuable. Not with a two-year contract that will have ZERO impact on your business.

SEO can't work now as it used to because:

- People are spending less time on websites and more time on social platforms like Facebook and Instagram.
- There is a lot of competition, and it has been going on for over 10 years. Facebook and Instagram advertising are newer than SEO.
- Even if you get first page, you'd be sixth under four or five Google paid ads for that keyword.
- Traffic from generic keywords is generic; we can't show it content the same way we can with Facebook ads (with retargeting strategies, etc.).
- Not only is the competition higher than the prices, but your ad will appear next to five others, all relatable to yours.

However, I want to tell you something. If you are not a sanitary professional, and instead are an agency owner or an agency freelancer:

Yes, you're going to make way more money off the client by selling SEO services than by selling Facebook ads.

With Facebook ads, if there are no results within four days, it's very unlikely that there will be any results at all.

You'll have to re-make the campaigns over and over again, spending money in the process.

With SEO, what you do isn't this trackable; if you block your client into a two-year contract with SEO, you can see the money pouring in and you're done.

With SEO, what you do is easy to fake. You can say, "Look, you're on the first page," for a keyword nobody really clicks, but you can make your clients believe that everybody does.

People made good money with SEO. Empires have been built upon fire-weaponry. Ink print probably caused the industrial revolution

However, just as I don't hang around dressed as an ancient Roman aristocrat, neither should you use SEO in 2019 for local health services. Most people doing SEO now have moved to Google ads or Facebook ads or whatever.

CHAPTER 5

You want to be an aesthetic dentist: Doctor Apa case study

Analysis of Dr. Apa's Instagram page and personal brand

Aesthetic dentist Dr. Michael Apa has one of the greatest Instagram pages at the moment. We'll examine how it is managed so that you can level up yours. I suggest that you follow him on Instagram (@doctorapa) and give the page a look before reading this chapter.

If you don't have Instagram, search on Google for "doctorapa instagram". Give it a look.

First: I feel obliged to speak about Instagram for a moment. What is Instagram and how is it different from Facebook?

Facebook is where the old dudes are. There are plenty of them on Facebook. I know it all started as a young guy's thing, but actually, Facebook is where 50-year-olds are posting pictures of kittens. It's where my mom spends time stalking her old classmates. It's where the most lavish discussions of politics happen. When I was a teenager, we were on Instagram; now that I'm in my 30s, most people on Instagram are older than I am.

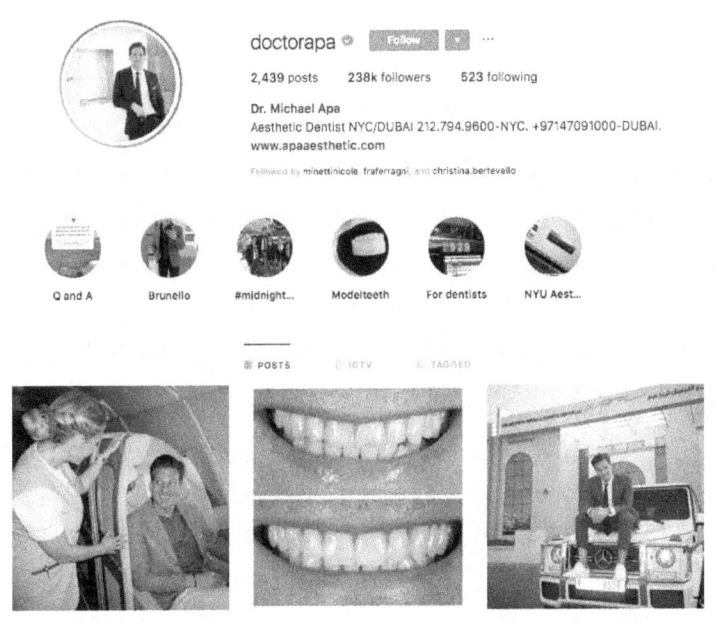

Sixty-two percent of online seniors aged 65+ are on Facebook, while 72% are between 50-64.

Most 50+ people spend time on the Facebook platform (hours a day) yet they don't know how to use it very well. They don't know how to properly reply to a comment, how to distinguish an ad from an organic, real post. On

Facebook, most seniors can't distinguish real news from fake news. Most people who comment on posts don't even click on the link before sharing the comment; thus, they are commenting on something they haven't fully evaluated. *(For more, see: "6 out of 10 will share this link without reading it." from the Washington Post Jul 16, 2016)*

So, most young guys aren't on Facebook for various reasons. It is where they'll be stalked if they are applying for a job. It is where people will see pics of them that they didn't want to be shared. There are 2 kinds of young girls:

1. Those who don't have Facebook
2. Those who have Facebook, but don't use it

Although we are dramatising here, I refer you to 2 articles from The Guardian: *"Teens are abandoning Facebook in dramatic numbers, study finds"* and *"Is Facebook for old people? Over 55s flock in as the young leave."* You'll find links to these articles at the end of this book, among the references.

Obviously, there are girls on Facebook, and Facebook has 2.3 billion users. What I'm telling you here is how the platforms are evolving. Instagram is a new platform with some features that make it more appealing to a younger audience.

1. The Instagram algo hasn't reached the level of Facebook's. If you post something on Instagram,

chances are that somebody will actually see it even if you haven't paid for it. The same is not true for Facebook. As you might have noticed, if you post something on Facebook, especially from a page, and get 3 likes, you're kind of a celebrity. But I have good news for you; this isn't happening because you're not popular anymore or you got ugly. It's just Facebook's algo giving precedence to paid posts – something not happening on this scale on Instagram. On Instagram, people get likes and followers more easily than they do on Facebook.

2. On the Instagram platform, you can choose any name you want and you can easily set it up as private. For example, your Uncle Thomas won't necessarily see your bikini selfies (if you're a girl) or your beer nights.

3. Instagram is a platform where aesthetics plays a bigger role. Instagram is not the place for commenting on politics. This makes it a better place for some people. Precedence is given to images.

Today our emphasis is on aesthetics and girls, not because I own, among my businesses, a bikini brand. (We sold another brand we owned to a German tech company but that's for another book.) If you are an aesthetic dentist, or an aesthetic surgeon, or you sell a tooth whitening powder or a weight-loss product, Instagram is absolutely, in 2019, the place to be.

Again, in 2026 I don't know, but in 2019, if you're not heavily advertising on Instagram, reaching 10,000 people per post, with an average of at least 1,000 likes per post, you're wasting time and money.

And opportunities.

The longer you wait, the more the platform will be saturated and the more you might be penalized by an algorithm change toward the Facebook trend (which is: you pay, I show the posts).

If you are treating anything aesthetic-related, go with it, even if your treatment is geared toward older women. Don't try to "understand" anything. Post a picture, make sure it looks nice, place some hashtags related to the subject. Done.

Don't post pictures with excessive text or filters. Use real images, in high definition, that show authentic moments. Look for who is doing well in your niche and adapt this to yourself. Don't try to reinvent the wheel.

If you're a cosmetic dentist, look at Dr. Apa's Instagram page (@doctorapa).

Instagram will help you do three things:

1. Sell your treatments.
2. Create a community of fans/followers who will actually see what you post <u>for free</u>. (Not like on

Facebook. Our Celest Bikini page on Facebook has around 40,000 followers. If we post something, we organically reach around 32 people. Not a good start.) On Instagram, the more engaged your followers are with what you post, the more they will see. Even on Instagram, if you have 100 followers, not all 100 will see your post, if not because they looked directly for you. In the good old days when all this started, they all saw your posts. Opportunities on the internet have to be captured quickly. Believe me, we won't have the same platforms in the next 10 years.

3. Make yourself look like a celebrity. Guess what? If you work in aesthetics, the more you look like a celebrity, the better for you and your prices. YOU DON'T WANT TO LOOK CHEAP – NOT IN REAL LIFE AND NOT ON INSTAGRAM.

To develop an Instagram page, you have to invest time and energy into it, as well as have a long-term mindset. When I started Celest Bikini, Instagram was the only choice.

We hammered on it for 4 years, seeking an audience that is very close to yours. Our consumer is very receptive to any cosmetic treatment, to the point that we developed campaigns that defended the right of any woman to get plastic surgery whenever she wanted.

It made a huge noise and we were featured on online gossip pages. We got people insulting us and people defending us. What matters is that our strongest fan base received content that represented them, while polarizing other kinds of content that weren't relevant to us. We don't sell to everybody, and neither should you.

If a girl has had breast augmentation, it is very likely that she will like our brand. This is something expressed in our communication and content every day. Not by chance, but because we strategize it. So should you (obviously at different levels).

Doctor Apa has one of the best pages on Instagram. Other dentists may have more followers but some of them have strong backgrounds in TV. I wanted to isolate and choose somebody whose efforts on the platform played a bigger role in determining his popularity than his efforts outside of the platform. The Kardashians have been on TV since I was a child, while influencers like Chiara Ferragni came out of nothing. So we chose Michael because he has done it without leaked porn videos (sorry, Kim Kardashian).

From our Instagram Page @Celest_Bikini

P.S.: What is an influencer and who is Chiara Ferragni?
An "influencer" is what you should be as a doctor, e.g.,

somebody who influences, through their own behaviour, other people on the internet. Chiara Ferragni, if you wish to check, is one of the best in the world at the moment.

She's not a doctor; she started as a fashion blogger.

Moreover, I suggest that you combine online and offline efforts. You are not an e-commerce; Instagram has to be there and work in a system with all your other marketing channels.

I see most guys in healthcare handing down social passwords to any assistant/secretary and telling them, "Take care of it." Then they move on to buying some unnecessary health equipment they got sold into purchasing.

Look, no patient ever walked into a clinic because of its health equipment. Either you're based in Burundi or everyone expects the same level of efficiency in all clinics. Your walls and the way your assistant presents you, your online presence: all these play a bigger role. You paid thousands for the equipment but you failed to tell your patients why it's better equipment. So what's the point?

You'd better regain control of your online presence and start from there, especially if you're selling aesthetic treatments. Doctor Apa could have goats and cows in his clinic eating grass off the ground and people would still think he's top of the game. Why? Because of his online presence and his personal brand.

If it were really about buying the best equipment, then any moron with access to credit could make billions in healthcare. IT'S NOT about that and I urge you to stop focusing your energy on buying the next thing or attending the next technical seminar or whatever. Focus on yourself and what you communicate

You know what? Buying expensive stuff, hiring somebody you don't really need – it makes you look like you're working. It produces no results and can lead you to ruin but it makes you look very busy. I've been into it myself. However, looking busy won't help you get to the next level, even though it can make you feel ok with yourself and the people surrounding you.

What makes Doc Apa's profile stand out?

I could talk about this for ages. The first thing is authentic content. The second thing is frequently updated content.

Most health content on the internet isn't authentic at all. People are presented as pieces of meat. You know what I'm talking about, especially if you're a dentist. Most doctors communicate on the internet as if they're speaking to other doctors, but they should be advertising to their patients, not their classmates.

Authentic content means you're exposing yourself and showing what your life is about after you finish work. It means showing yourself when you're not at 100% just because you have to. It means sharing what keeps you awake, what makes you proud. It's not easy.

Most people, even outside healthcare, are very reluctant to show themselves. So we have clinics with no face and that must advertise using other leverage. If you can't establish a brand, you'll soon find yourself competing for Walmart prices.

You'd better show your face, even if it's not the prettiest. The more human you look, the better it will be for you as a doctor and as a professional. By saying this, I don't mean you have to be a dummy in front of the camera and play a role. I see tons of this, too

Maybe a boss pushes his or her employees to put their faces into what they do, and here we have some fake-happy moments in the office or in the clinic. To work, it has to be real. Make it authentic.

Doc Apa's profile is full of authentic moments. Traveling, cars, eating, having fun. Being an aesthetic doc in a crowded, expensive market, he knows you can't look cheap. If you want to magnetize the wealthiest, you won't be able to do it by looking cheap.

I still see important doctors not flying private, not showing their cars or watches because they are afraid of what people might think about them. But I'll tell you something: There is no successful man or woman who cares about what other people think. Not even in healthcare.

Doctor Apa manages to be candid in every picture and can show you how a personal brand must be a mix of clinical cases and personal life. I see surgeons posting before-and-after photos ALL DAY LONG. Man, they look good, but they are not what sells. They're hooks, but you can't get on a ring with only hooks. Boxing, you need jab, jab, jab and then a hook. *(See Gary V.'s book,* Jab Jab, Right Hook*, for the importance of creating marketing content that is not geared toward making a direct sale on your product.)*

People buy based on emotions, People accept a treatment when they are moved by emotion. Emotions help in situations when you can recognize yourself in the seller. If you spark that connection, all defenses are laid down. That's why you need your patients to want to be you. Before-and-after pictures are part of the game; they must be there, but don't focus only on them. Think of the story

Would you really tell a story 10,000 times with a black canvas, in profile, every day – day after day? What kind of story is that?

The moral of the story might always be the same, but stories have to be varied.

I love how Apa mixes shots of daily life; it makes you fall in love with what he does. The average dentist has some A or B celebrity come in and will just upload the same old fake photos of both of them smiling. Doctor Apa has comedians from the internet come in and do viral gags with him in his studio.

The average dentist does NO interviews; they use lavish phrases involving the word "smile." "Smile" is a saturated word in your world. Apa has some interview extracts, just a few words and phrases, but they make a big impact. You don't even need to know who asked those questions and where. They're just quotes.

And yet most clinic owners have the "free visit" marketing. They can do better.

I chose this case study because most photos on Apa's Instagram are real pictures, and you can do the same with a mobile. Some pictures on Apa's profile are underexposed, others need a bit of Photoshop. However, if he can look good with no Photoshop, no filters, you can too. Stop posting only before-and-after pictures.

Most of the aesthetic professionals I know are into the same things their patients are. If you're into cosmetics, you probably like Audemars Piguet and Michelin Starred Restaurants. If you can afford to spend $12,000 on enhancing your smile, it is very likely that you'll be impressed by my private flights and celebrity friends and patients. I see professionals having all this, yet hiding it.

It's not showing off and you ought to stop worrying that people will think you're Paris Hilton. And by the way, I've met Paris personally in Milan and she's a beautiful person.

Apa's fascination with Brunello Cucinelli (whom I had the pleasure of meeting and hanging out with at PITTI Florence when I worked in fashion) gives him deeper personality traits, as does the fact that he lives between Dubai and New York. Mental associations work.

Apa's being close to an Italian fashion stylist like Cucinelli, in our minds, links the two of them. These links are the roots of a personal brand.

If you sell high-ticket treatments, you should communicate "high-ticket." If you sell high-ticket cosmetic services, you might consider having some famous names come to your clinic for free. You don't need 1,000. You need just one Victoria Secret's Angel and it's like you've got all of them. P.S. You can contact a modeling agency and arrange something with them if you have no contacts.

Apa's life is essentially a celebrity life. And, yes, if you want to be an aesthetic dentist, you have to be a celebrity. It will be a lot more about your vision than about your equipment, where you come from, and who your father and mother are.

Once you have the vision, you'll need somebody to document your life day to day, as if you were on a reality show. Here, we're not talking about handing over social media passwords to your assistant's assistant. We are talking about building a brand around a personality. A personal brand.

We are talking about making you a celebrity.

As with any celebrity, emphasis must be placed on the voice. Your voice, Apa's voice … any celebrity has a strong, recognizable voice. You hear it a few times and you never forget it.

Apa's YouTube channel is a treasure of inspiration. It's mouth-opening. It's better than a TV show. The editing, the sound, the music – everything is perfect. Do yourself a favour and check it out.

Maybe you're not living Doctor Apa's life but I've noticed that most of my clients, while living very interesting lives, were hiding them. The fact that you travel with your kids, your accent, your lifestyle, the restaurants you visit: All this plays a big role in establishing your personal brand.

In health, there are no shortcuts. Either you create a brand around yourself, your image, your persona, or you will have to create a brand around a name, a clinic, a chain, an "entity." There is no shortcut. When you open a new space, you invest in equipment, staff, overhead. How much do you invest every year in authority, image, personal branding?

What successful people do to be successful is under everyone's eye, every day. You have it. There is no secret thing that successful healthcare professionals do that you can't see. It's simply about getting rid of the limiting beliefs that make you do things as 90% of the market does.

CHAPTER 6

You want to be an implantology master: Doctor Saverio Ferrari Parabita case study

Analysis of Dr. Saverio Ferrari Parabita's television presence and personal brand

S omething you don't know about me: There is a guy who taught me a lot. To be honest, there are many. My dad and my mom. My grandmother, my grandfather. Dan Kennedy, Frank Merenda, Sam Ovens, Russell Brunson, Tai Lopez, Grant Cardone, Dan Lok, Niccolò Pocchini, Piernicola de Maria, Beatrice Blandino. But one guy taught me something that might interest you more.

And it relates more to you. That guy is Saverio Ferrari Parabita. He's a surgeon who does advanced implantology. He is one of the most important dentists in Italy (and in the world) and has been mentoring me since I started this journey.

He has built a reputation as an authority in what he does. He didn't teach me anything about online marketing, yet he's one of the best teachers I've had in my life. If he creates a mentoring program about himself, dentists would have to pay at least $100,000 to attend.

Needless to say, he's a pro in surgery, but that's not enough and it's not the point. I will speak to you about his personal brand. What he does is less aesthetic than veneers and more functional; he mastered what most dentists in Italy are afraid to (or cannot) do: treating patients who are missing mouth bone.

Saverio

These kinds of treatments need a savvy hand and not just anybody can do them. Patients who have lost all the bone face a huge problem: Where am I going to place the implants? As you might know, mouth bone without teeth tends to retreat, creating the infamous "old" look on some unlucky faces you might have seen.

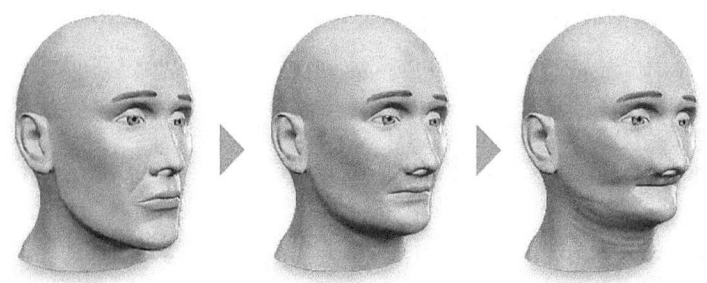

The infamous "old" look

Patients who face this situation have had difficult life journeys that have led to the current state of their mouths.

These are cases that most dentists in Italy don't want. However, Saverio, through his personal branding, his research, and his studies, has become a specialist in this.

There are many lessons to learn from Saverio, who, through the internet, has amplified his personal brand and propagated his message on an industrial scale.

The first lesson for you:

What's the point of university awards?

I have clients who have attended university masters, received awards, made speeches, won prizes. And their patients don't know about it.

So, what's the point? For your mom to know it? For your friends to know it?

You should communicate, to all your patients, what you're studying, what you're teaching as a professor.

And yes, you have to be a professor, not just a doctor.

You want to be the most experienced person in the nation on that subject. However, that alone isn't enough.

You must be the most experienced person in your patients' eyes.

Being the most experienced in the loneliness of your study room won't boost the perception your potential patients have of you. Everybody needs to know that you are the most experienced.

Obviously, you can't do this by speaking one-on-one with the patient. You don't just greet them and say, "You know, I made this, I made that, I'm so good, etc."

They need to know it; it has to be indirect, and they need to be reminded of it by different channels.

The role of the master, the professor, is the strongest role you can have as a human being.

I've had clients who worked hard to win awards, give speeches, attend events, study at masters, and yet the only way they were communicating this was through a post on Facebook or something hanging from a wall in an inconspicuous part of their office.

The fact you post something on Facebook might help your conscience but it is not helping your wallet and your personal brand. I've had clients whose eyes have popped out of their heads, telling me, "Yes, we are going to post this, and next week that, on our Facebook page, and we got these likes and these comments," as if they were Beyoncé on stage in front of hundreds of thousands of people. They're not.

That is not doing your job. Nobody cares. Actually, it's not that nobody cares; instead, to care, you first have to see it. If your Facebook post reaches 32 people in its lifetime, you are lucky if you get 2 clicks and a few likes. When we promote posts on Facebook or Instagram, we try to reach around 1,00,000 people, at least in areas that are not crowded (I'm not talking about New York).

You have to research, to build your network and knowledge. But why are you doing this in secret? It must be CLEAR and it must be BROADCASTED.

I'm talking about something more than hanging your degree on a wall. You're probably doing everyday stuff that would add so much to your personal brand, if you only had a vision for it. For a second, stop seeing the world through a doctor's eyes and instead see it through a patient's eyes.

Being an authority will multiply your referral rate tenfold. It means that people will speak more about you and suggest you more, even if you did not actually visit with them.

There's a difference between being presented as "Oh, go there, he's got good prices" and being presented as "You have to meet with him, he's the top in this field."

You want the authority to dictate the treatment, the price, the timing. This authority is communicated through the books you publish, the appearances you make on TV, your online presence, the conventions where you present, the events you attend, your past experience in hospitals or foreign countries, the awards you win.

What's the point of all this? You want to be perceived as the only option when one thinks of your field. How do you achieve this? I repeat:

- TV appearances (not TV commercials, but interviews on scientific health programs)
- Patients' testimonials
- Book publications
- In-clinic footage of you operating
- In-clinic videos of you presenting new technologies, new solutions, new everything
- Work in universities, awards, research
- Interviews in newspapers and magazines

What's the point of doing this if somebody is already doing it in your area and is already bombing the internet with this content? It means you might be coming in late.

It means you come in second, or even third.

If there are 3 of you, you're not going to divide the pie into 3 equal slices.

The first who bites into the pie takes 90% of it.

If you are often interviewed on TV about implantology or whatever your niche is, you'll get the attention of (in the case of regional TV) around 150,000 people.

But you get it once. You don't build a brand from one TV appearance! You build a brand in a lifetime.

With the internet, we can get those 150,000 to see your ads, and I decide when and how many times. And you have TV authority, yet not the narrow broadcast. You can broadcast it 3 times a day. You can broadcast it to 1,500,000 people.

Come late into a market where we are already playing this game, and we are playing it with your competitor. You're going to get a very little piece of the pie.

You're going to eat the crumbs.

If you work in trichology in Texas, you want to own that word on people's minds. People in Texas must think of your name when they think of hair treatments.

You have to own your word, first in your vision and then in your patient's mind. It works regionally. You don't have to own it throughout the world. If you're in Texas, you own it in Texas. If you're in Lebanon, you own it in Lebanon. But damn, you better own it.

If trichology is already taken, you take another one, and you make a 15-year (at least) plan for that word, and that process, and you build a brand around it. If trichology is taken, you can work on a sub-category of trichology.

And you'd better put yourself in that brand, put your personality into it. People want to see that too, and they are going to choose you based on it.

If you want to be like Saverio, an implantology master, a professor, you don't have to reinvent the wheel. The 'professor' archetype is already in your patient's mind. And I'll tell you something: You might have competitors who already play that role.

But you know what? Once they're playing their role one-on-one within their clinic walls, they're harmless.

When you play that role, and you can broadcast it to 100,000-1,000,000 people in your area, and you do it for years..

Then what? <u>You become the best at what you do.</u>

Not for what you actually did, but for who you're perceived to be, for your reputation.

Not for who you really are or for who your colleagues think you are but for who your patients think you are.

Your colleagues' perception of you could be the total opposite of what the average patient thinks … and you know what? Your colleagues are your competitors and you're magnetizing wealth from them to yourself. That's why they might not like you. Their opinion doesn't matter.

Who your patients think you are: Nothing on earth matters more. Who your potential patients think you are: You need nothing more than that.

Let's say you don't have the money for TV. How can we do it? With online, we can broadcast that message to more people, many more times, at a cheaper price. This is for now, in 2019, if you take action today. I don't know if it will be the same in the future. The opportunity for digital marketing in healthcare is now.

To be that person, you need courage, as Saverio had (and has). You need to be persistent. But once you're that person, you're done.

Whenever we work with somebody like Saverio, somebody who already has his own direction, somebody who has already developed his charismatic character, the process is much easier.

You take all the best patients and the rest of the market goes to the cheapest solutions. You have 2 markets: 1 is Saverio for those who can and want to afford it, while the other is low-cost clinics.

To fill a patient market, a niche, you must think of yourself as huge. There must be space for only 2: (1) you and (2) those who can't afford you.

The speech

I was impressed by Saverio's speech when I first saw it on TV, the way he speaks to the core of his patients.

He's no average dentist or surgeon, speaking about technical stuff. He goes straight to the heart, and his speeches cover everything about what patients feel.

He discusses the high prices they might not be able to afford, while most of his colleagues waver and change the subject when the topic of price comes up.

He discusses the fears of not understanding what he's talking about.

He shows enthusiasm for a new revolutionary technique that he knows will change the lives of thousands.

Being a sanitary professional, a surgeon, a dentist, is such a blessing. You don't work in finance, making rich people richer. You don't make a living touching buttons on a screen or enduring office diatribes.

You change people's lives.

You do it every day; the magic is already happening and you're losing sight of it. If you give hair back to a bald man, you will change the way women look at him when he enters a club.

If you give teeth back to a 60-year-old, you are fixing his self-esteem, his personal life, the way his sons look at and think about him.

You are changing their lives. Your Instagram and Facebook page is probably full of pointless photos of your dental chairs, a picture of you with your arms crossed, and (if you're a pro) some before-and-after shots with a black background. Are you looking at the finger or are you looking at the moon?

On a TV program, Saverio has 6 testimonials from those whose lives he has changed. We are broadcasting the show across the internet: YouTube, Facebook, Instagram. Millions of people reached.

We are showing it multiple times for those who have more interest in it. Dozens of times.

And for those who watched it and didn't book an appointment? We'll have them watch another broadcast.

And another. Until what? Until they book an appointment.

Can this apply to you? Yes.

It can now, before somebody else does it. Before you have an agency that wants you to do SEO.

Max Arnaudo

This is not SEO; this is changing people's lives for the better.

It means you're a hero and we are celebrating this every day.

You profit, the patient's life is changed. What a job have you, and you don't even know it.

One day

The first day I met Saverio, I went to his office and pitched my offer. I told him the great results we were having and I saw that Saverio and Fulvia (his colleague) were very interested.

They asked me intelligent questions and I provided very detailed answers. At the end of the speech, after over an hour of speaking, they told me, "Ok, just send me an email and we'll look into it."

Which is similar to your patients saying, "I will let you know."

Or to the time when, in high school, girls weren't answering your SMSs (we had SMS and not WhatsApp at the time) or calls.

Which means: *'no, thank you'*

128

As a child, you hear "no" often and you have to obey. However, I believe that when you are an adult, you should never take no for an answer.

Successful people don't do that, and if you're reading this book, chances are you want to be successful. Maybe you already are. Chances are you get what I mean when I say that I don't take no for an answer.

So I stayed there and I kept insisting. I had seen the incredible amount of content that Saverio already had; I had seen the way he spoke on video. I knew it would have been impossible to not deliver amazing results to him.

I had to. If I couldn't with him, I couldn't with anybody else (and we were already doing it with people who had little content!).

So I told him that my dream, my goal in life, is to own a bank before I'm 50 years old. This has been my dream since I was a teenager. I have always wanted a bank and I'm going to own one before I'm 50 years old.

Saverio told me, "My friend has a bank too, it's nothing special."

I answered, "I don't mean sitting in an office down the street, lending money to lease cars. I mean doing a hostile takeover of one of the biggest banks in the country. When I say I want to own a bank, I mean I want to control Unicredit (i.e., Italy's biggest bank, one of the largest in the world).

Saverio understood how crazy I am, and understood that I wasn't there for a quick buck; I was there to play the game. I cared about the results. So he gave me the money to start.

Later the next week he told me that he had given me that money because I had stirred an emotion within him. Then he taught me something I will always take with me, and you'd better take it with yourself, to your grave:

People choose based on their emotions, and on how they relate to you. *The best way to spark emotions and illustrate who you are is through stories.*

Keep this in mind when you show a patient any treatment plan. The reasons why someone wants a new smile, bigger breasts, to hear again: these are MUCH more profound than you can imagine.

Think about this the next time you market a "free visit" or some "also open Saturdays" offer. Or before doing SEO. Think emotions.

Digital gives you the best tools to broadcast stories. Stories reveal emotions and content, which are opportunities that can change your life.

CHAPTER 7

How digital marketing can place a hospital at the top of its patients' minds

Acquiring patients while building a brand

P atients use hospital services infrequently but when they have to do so, you want your structure to be on top of their list. For your hospital to position itself in your future patients' minds, your marketing strategy should focus more on building a brand and less on short-term results.

Direct marketing is the field of marketing that specializes in having your audience take an action after they consume your content. You want them to buy your burger now with a coupon, to call you to book a chiro appointment, or to take immediate advantage of your carpet cleaning promotion.

With a hospital, this is not possible. People go to hospitals only when they have to. While your structure might be the prettiest on earth, in most situations, the less a person visits it, the happier they are.

But you still want your structure to be at the top of the list. There are a few things we need to acknowledge first.

<u>People form opinions about hospitals based on their relatives' and co-workers' opinions, or on first-hand experience</u>. We can build the biggest hype about your structure and have Oprah, Ellen, Leonardo DiCaprio, and Beyoncé promote it, yet all that money is flushed down the drain if the experience doesn't match the hype.

Because we must be concerned about patient satisfaction when we promote hospitals, online serves as a tool not only for creating an immediate economic return (with campaigns dedicated to acquiring patients <u>now</u>) but also for both creating a brand and checking its value based on patients' perceptions.

If you're a trichologist in Turkey and you work with Patient-Acquisition.Com , we'll focus mainly on bringing people from Europe to your clinic. Full stop. But if you're a local hospital, different strategies apply. A hospital needs a long-term brand awareness program. Hospital marketing must be reliant on operations. If facilities aren't clean enough, if the staff is rude and treatments perceived as low-quality, no online advertising can save your structure.

At the same time, if you focus on brand perception over a long enough span, you'll be on top of the list among other hospitals that might have better equipment, more easily accessible location, bigger structure and so on.

You need digital marketing as a tool, first and foremost, to assess the current perception of your brand and your operations.

Let's lay down how you should use online for hospital marketing, listed in order of importance:

1. Brand building over a long-term span
2. Checking feedback about staff, facilities, treatment value perception, and the overall brand
3. Internet campaigns that bring patients to your door immediately (we'll see some examples later)
4. Optimize processes (CRMs, booking online, waiting times, etc.)
5. Retain patients

1. Brand Building

You need a brand because a hospital is made to last. Part of your efforts should be geared toward building authority around your structure, and that is something built over the years.

While fancy facilities might have an impact on the first days, when you're managing a hospital, there is no possibility of cheating; any staff failure, any rudeness, any time the structure defaults – that information is broadcast by word of mouth in your local area.

In this situation, brand building can't be something you just assign to agencies or marketing departments. Rather, it must be an effort that stems from the entire structure. How front offices answer the phone, how the cleaning staff operates, how nurses and doctors relate to patients: All your marketing is here, first and foremost.

How you build the processes that bring people taking certain actions in certain ways is at the core of your hospital brand-building effort. How you assess these processes monthly and how you build a culture around what you do is the vital point.

Once this thing that you created exists internally, we can communicate it online, at a cheaper price, telling stories every day, for years. However, these stories must match the reality. And people know.

The use of testimonials and the propagation of success stories online should be done weekly and showcased using video equipment. The more you propagate this process over months, the more you build a brand. During the brand-building process, the hospital should never be the one talking about how good it is; rather, this is the patients' job.

The shift from promoting the structure itself to speaking about health-related topics that are relevant to patients' needs is the second pillar for building a brand around a hospital. Online is the best tool; there, you can propagate infinite content and be sure that people will see it. You can't provide such content on fast-lane advertising billboards or on newspaper pages. It would not fit.

Webinars (live videos with MDs speaking about health topics) are a great way to create a database of people interested in such topics. Potential patients will unconsciously choose your structure as the go-to one for that particular topic. Thanks to a Customer Relationship Management tool, you'll soon find that people attending webinars will be hospitalized in your structure.

Webinar, or Web Conferencing consists of a seminar conducted over the internet, where people attend in real time for the first registration. The conversion rate of webinars is higher than the one of simple videos broadcasted on the internet, thus the increasing use of them in all over the world

---

Customer Relationship Manager or CRM is a strategy for managing an organisation's relationships and interactions with customers and potential customers. When people talk about CRM, they are usually referring to a CRM system, a tool that is used for contact management, sales management, productivity, and more

The more information you provide for your patients' starving minds, the higher you will rank in those minds when it comes to choosing you. This information is the same information your staff gives to your patients one-on-one during visits, yet broadcasting them on the internet gives you the authority and the awareness your brand needs.

2. Feedback

The internet is where everybody shares their thoughts, especially when those thoughts aren't sought and especially when those thoughts are not relevant. Yet everybody does it. A study showed that, after relatives and friends, <u>random comments on the internet are the most trusted source of information for patients who must make a decision</u>.

We already know that most people comment on online newspaper articles without reading them, based only on the headings. We live in a world where people leave comments about information they didn't read (probably written by journalists who didn't research well, either). What matters to us today is that this information, no matter how marginal or false it is, has become increasingly important and relevant to our patients.

We are aware, rationally, that one can have terrible reviews and still be an amazing hospital. However, if we ourselves were checking out that hospital, we would skip it, not only as patients but as a network. If a client asks to work with us and we see very poor reviews about the client's structure, our desire to accept the job decreases.

Yet these reviews might not reflect the truth. *They are not "the truth".* But they are an enough trustable source of perceptions. And perceptions are what, lastly, matter.

These might be false reviews. Or one wrong hire at the front desk might be the cause. Maybe just one person wrote several reviews. Maybe the problem has been fixed. Doesn't matter, as long as the reviews are easily accessible, and they can be perceived as trustable, the perception lasts.

There is a huge difference between real value and perception. However, you might find, in reading this book, that all decisions—mine, yours—are based on perception.

Online surveys are a necessary tool for investigating and eradicating whatever is causing problems in your structure. The bigger and complex the structure the bigger you need to evaluate it daily with online surveys.

It might be just one person or one division causing the entire structure to collapse. Fortunately, as people are not afraid of sharing their opinions online, I'd suggest finding out (anonymously and online) who is complaining about your structure. These are not your enemies but your friends. Change the way you see them.

Tip: you can create an automated alert on google so that when somebody speaks some chosen keywords about you on the internet, you'll be notified. Check www.google.com/alerts for more

You must assess both potential patients and actual patients. While most people wouldn't dare complain in front of a nurse or doctor, they still might have had a terrible experience. The fact that they won't complain in front of the staff doesn't mean they won't do it online, with their relatives, or with their friends, forever.

The internet is the best tool for assessing and checking on how you're doing. This is because it offers anonymity and because you can reach hundreds of thousands of people in one day. You can actually "measure" your brand's perception over the months using a low-budget campaign with enough statistical inference.

A survey on "how we did" also shows that you care. This is better than stating, yourself, that you're "the best hospital in your city."

3. Short-term campaigns (for <u>immediate</u> patient acquisition)

Hospitals are divided into departments. Because all departments are different, we can agree that one campaign bringing in generic "patients" would have no point.

You need a campaign for every department—or better yet, at least one campaign for every high-ticket treatment.

Most hospitals promote "Breast Cancer Awareness Month." This is good except for the fact that if that month is promoted by all hospitals, you'll be doing what everyone else is doing—not the smartest decision

We'll take, as an example, how Chris Boyer is leading Inova Hospital social media marketing. It's an excellent example of a great ad for drawing patients to a hospital

Here's the ad:

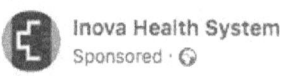 **Inova Health System**
Sponsored · 🌐

An estimated 83.6 million American adults have one or more types of CVD or cardiovascular disease. Learn about various risk factors and discover what steps that one can take to improve heart health.

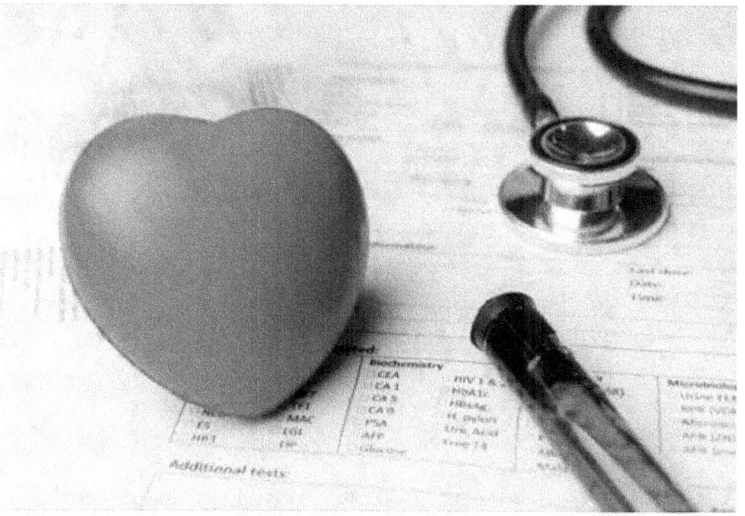

INOVA.ORG
Take A FREE Heart Risk Assessment   [Learn More]
Learn about the risk factors by taking Inova's FREE hea...

That brings the visitor to a landing page. (Note that this is a specific landing page, not the hospital website's homepage.):

Heart and Vascular Institute

Heart Risk Assessment

What's your heart age? Take this free online heart health risk assessment to find out.

You'll be able to: Compare your actual age to your heart's biological age, calculate your risk of developing cardiovascular disease, prioritize your most harmful cardiovascular risk factors and more.

Begin My Assessment

Are you at risk for heart disease? Is your blood pressure too high? Are your cholesterol levels in the proper range? Taking this assessment can help you find out that and more including:

Compare
Compare your actual heart age to your heart's biological age

Prioritize
Learn how you can minimize your most harmful risk factors

When you click to "begin my assessment," you are taken to a page like this:

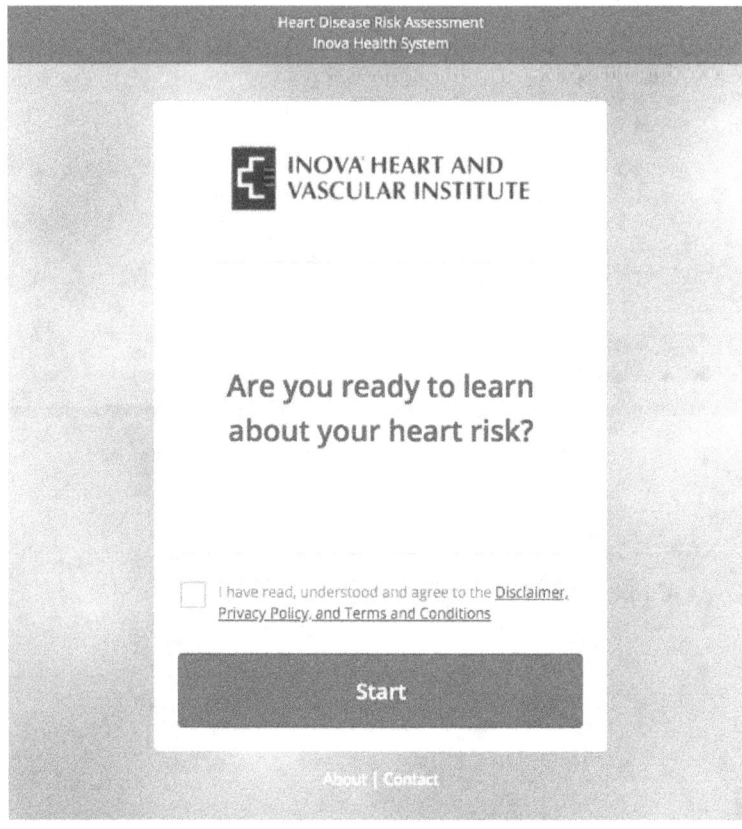

This is a quiz. What is the scope of a quiz like this?

1. Gather information about the potential patient. This information goes straight to your CRM.
2. Skim through who is not really interested. (If they don't fill out a form, would they care to pay?)

3. Have them book an appointment with your hospital.

You're never too young—or too old—to take care of your heart. Congratulations on taking an important step toward heart health today.

Age

60

Sex

⬤ Male

◯ Female

Height

6   1

Weight

Note how the copy on the quiz has been written to persuade and influence the reader.

In an automated way, you can assess your patient's situation before you even see them one on one. This helps reduce costs and optimize the process.

Have you experienced a **transient ischemic attack** (TIA or "mini-stroke")? ?

○ Yes

● No

Indicate if you have had any of these stroke symptoms.

(check all that apply)

☑ Weak, numb, or drooping hand, tongue, cheek, face, arm or leg

☐ Difficulty speaking, garbled/slurred speech, or inability to speak

☐ Blurred, doubled, or decreased vision in one or both eyes

☐ None of these

ONLINE PATIENT ACQUISITION PATIENTS

Then, page after page, after all the questions have been answered (from diabetes to blood pressure), we come to the results:

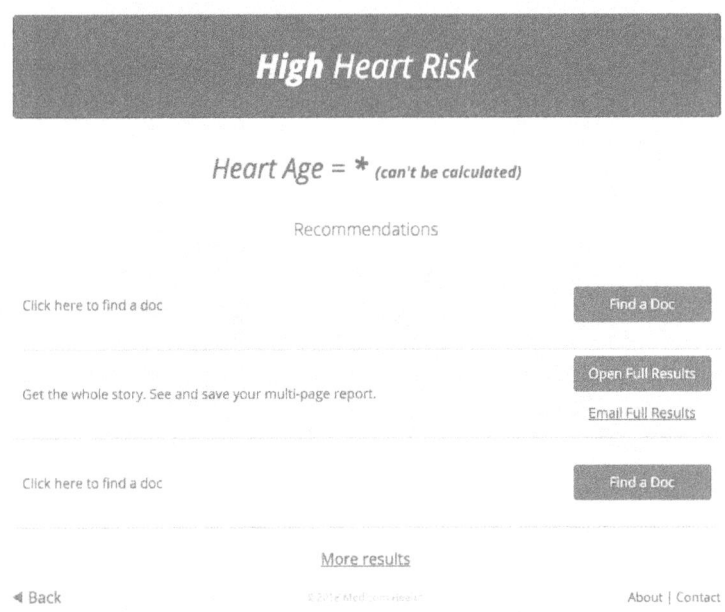

That clearly results in the patient finding a doctor (in your hospital) or reading the full report, which has been created to inform and persuade the reader to take action.

The reader is then:

- In your CRM so that you will be able to track his actions forever.

- Signed up for an email sequence with follow-ups, aimed at having the reader book an appointment.
- Retargeted through Facebook Advertising for the next few months.

The report (page 1 of 6):

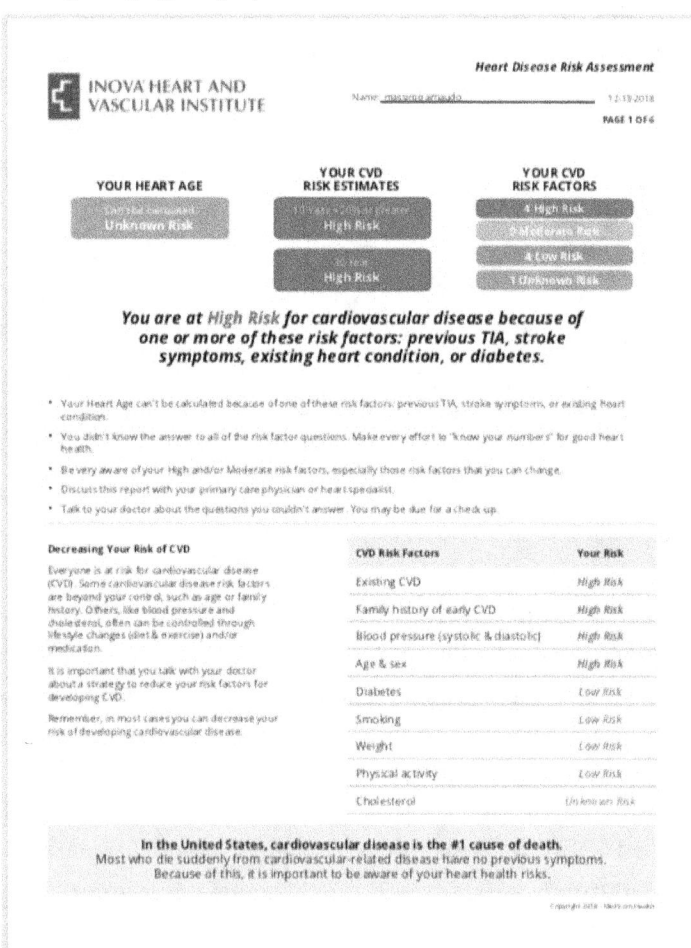

Copyright Medicom Health 2018

These same processes can be used for any niche your hospital treats.

4. Optimize processes

Whether it's beer delivered in self-driving trucks (which is happening now) or drones delivering Amazon products, technology is replacing most processes involving human attention. This is affecting healthcare too, but how?

CRM means customer relationship management, though in our industry it would be better to call it PRM: patient relationship management. PRM allows the health marketer to micro-target campaigns and reports so specifically that one can track every individual prospect.

Simply speaking, PRM means that instead of driving mass traffic to the hospital website, you can segment and create a different journey (involving SMS, emails, phone calls, and ad retargeting) for every potential and actual patient depending on their special needs. If we refer to the example in the last chapter, somebody opting in for a heart check will be followed before and after the treatment, receiving a different flow of content depending on the actions that they take. If they choose a treatment, they will be shown a certain type of content, while if they wait, they will be shown another. PRM can track patients to such a specific level that it can determine whether patients have read emails but not clicked on the links, or the number of seconds they spend looking at the content they're shown.

PRM is also good for "secret services," e.g., collecting data about a patient's personal life in such a way that your staff can relate to it on a deeper level. Think about trying to remember a patient's nephew's name six months after you saw that patient. This is now possible, automated and trackable, which results in a better experience for the patient and an easier procedure for the hospital staff. This software is easily accessible for smaller clinics, too.

Thanks to PRM, you can also track physician referral rate, thus creating and optimizing channels that bring patients to your hospital offline.

The digital revolution means that in addition to booking an appointment online, in certain situations you'll be able to visit patients online.

Hospitals like Inova offer a real-time "average waiting time" record for each structure. A recent study revealed that the satisfaction level of patients who had been waiting for hours but who received frequent updates containing "good" or "very good" information about the length of their waits was the same as that of patients waiting for just half an hour. *(Press Ganey)*

Neutralizing negative feedback and placing your hospital at the top of your patients' list is a priority that is easily attainable with digital marketing. Keeping promises will be a duty shared by everyone from the hospital's president to the front desk assistant.

CHAPTER 8

Selling products for patients online

From toothpaste to Viagra to hearing aids

I n this chapter, we'll dive into why some products or brands for patients are so successful on the internet and learn about the best ways to promote them depending on their niches.

We'll speak about Viagra and enhancing pills, hearing aids, HiSmileTeeth (a tooth whitening brand), and BOOM by Cindy Joseph (a pro-age beauty cream brand).

These four examples alone generate billions in sales every year through only the online market. Each is sold in a unique way. I left out classic e-commerce cases such as, for example, pharmacy websites. What makes these cases different and unique is the way in which patients are urged to buy the companies' products and not somebody else's.

Viagra and enhancing pills

Most of Viagra's success has come from the internet. In fact, the ability to buy it anonymously attracted most men who wouldn't dare buy it from their local pharmacies.

Some buyers may feel a sense of shame about buying enhancing pills (i.e., pills that promise to improve sexual life or enlarge male genitals). The industry might be considered a scam and has no proven deliverables. However the demand for such products is so high and visible over the internet that we couldn't refrain from talk about it.

A true need for penis enlargement surgery is rare. (A penis considered "micro" would be seven centimeters long when fully erect, yet would not require surgery.) However, patients' perception of the issue is one of the biggest yet least talked about matters.

Pornography and social stereotypes play a huge role in producing this situation, changing and re-shaping the ways in which people view sexuality. It has been scientifically proven that watching porn can cause addiction and that porn can be physically harmful to the male brain. However, as of the time of this writing, 30% of all data on the internet is porn, which has a huge, hidden impact on society.

As this is not the place for making judgments about moral character, we'll investigate the ways in which these products are sold on the internet.

Prescription drugs cannot be advertised on Facebook and are monitored on Google, which does not make it easy for Big Pharma to liberally promote its products. Often, patients buy prescription drugs online on e-commerce websites based in countries (especially in the EU) where no prescription is required.

Most of these products are sold online through SEO (as advertising them on paid channels would be difficult due to regulations), on <u>websites that look more like review sites than actual e-commerces</u>. These websites pretend to compare different products in a way that should communicate authority and trust. As we dive into these strategies I must point out one thing: In the case of enhancement pills, these strategies might lead to a scam of sorts.

Yet what's wrong here is not the strategy, which we can still use for a good cause. Rather, what's wrong is the intent behind it. You can—and should—use these strategies for good, though they might not have been used for that previously.

Superdrug.com   ▲ Register   **Sign in to your Account**

Browse our treatments

		4 tablets	8 tablets	12 tablets	16 tablets	28 tablets
	Viagra®	from £20.00	from £30.00	from £45.00	from £56.00	from £90.00
	Viagra Connect®	4 tablets £19.99	8 tablets £34.99	12 tablets £52.00	16 tablets £65.00	28 tablets £113.00
	Sildenafil	4 tablets from £18.00	8 tablets from £27.00	12 tablets from £40.50	16 tablets from £45.00	28 tablets from £78.00
	Cialis®	4 tablets from £44.00	8 tablets from £84.00	12 tablets from £120.00	16 tablets from £152.00	28 tablets from £285.00
	Tadalafil	4 tablets from £30.00	8 tablets from £50.00	12 tablets from £65.00	16 tablets from £85.00	28 tablets from £140.00

In this chapter, we'll see that <u>the practice of camouflaging actual e-commerce in blogs, news articles, and review sites is very common among those who sell products to patients online</u>. You rarely see fashion sold this way on the internet, but trust and authority are very important when one is selling these types of products (as they may interfere with your health). Thus, the following strategies apply.

I have personally seen (not through my own actions but through a fellow internet-marketer) that any ad promising a boost in virility attracts a huge amount of attention. At the same time, platforms like Facebook and Google get better every year at immediately recognizing and banning those who promote such content.

If you really had a product that could enhance a man's genitals without harming him, you'd have one of the most profitable companies in the world. Demand for these products is incredibly high. Yet, obviously, nobody talks about it.

An "advertorial" is an ad disguised as news. This strategy boosts any product's authority (whether legitimate or not) because someone else—not the advertiser—is speaking about the product.

Also, pop-ups (small windows that open without your consent while you browse the internet), combined with the usual banners, are a huge source of traffic for these products.

A promise, an appealing picture, a benefit, and a call to action: Here is your banner ad.

Speaking about this industry is necessary because it is the one taking the biggest share of the billion dollars pie.

Whether it is Viagra (which actually works), enhancing pills, or a cream that makes your beard or hair grow, enormous potential can be tapped online if you want to sell virility-related products. Anonymity, ease of buying, the persistence of the problem in people's lives: These all help make digital marketing the best platform for advertising such products. Whether you use these tools for good or bad is up to you. It's worth noting that as years passes, Facebook and Google get smarter at detecting such shady offers and ban them.

Enormous profits await for who will be able to sell these products giving actual, proven results and thus avoiding to be banned.

Hearing aids

Hearing aids are a great example of a product that must be sold using emotion-related leverage. The product itself (like Viagra) carries a strong stigma, indicating that its users are old or close to death. Opening a shop with "VIAGRA" written on its signboard and placing that shop in the middle of a crowded square won't help you sell more Viagra, even though the demand for such products is strong.

With hearing aids, the scenario is similar. The product is expensive (in this book, we refer only $1000+ hearing aids, although these items are experiencing an enormous competition from cheaper solutions) and embarrassing to wear, and nobody really wants to think about it.

Online, we can segment our campaigns, thus speaking to the direct user or relative. This can be done using different language and different types of emotional leverage depending on the case.

Although we suggest closing the sale of high-ticket products face to face, online can be your ally in giving your leads the content they require to make their decision. To sell them, we must address their objections BEFORE they visit us. You must perpetually automate and broadcast all this content on your customer screens, as their problem will not improve over the years.

Facebook advertising + CRM gives us the ability to target both the sons and the partners of the potential customer, thus presenting them with different messages over a long period of time.

These messages, sent *en masse*, will provide us with the big data we require to fix and optimize the machine. Here, by "machine" we mean the automated sending of content to our leads. Seeing what works and what doesn't, month by month, will allow us to adjust the machine and its messages.

Let's look at an example.

Mario's wife, Anna, is a 70-year-old housewife. One day she is scrolling through Facebook after lunch when she sees an article like this:

> "RETIREMENT HOME HOSPITALIZATIONS DROP NATIONALLY AS HEARING AIDS AND OTHER TECHNOLOGICAL ADVANCEMENTS GIVE SUBSTANTIAL INDEPENDENCE TO THEIR USERS"

The article captures Anna's attention. This is a new and different angle that she has never thought about. In everyone's mind, hearing aids are an embarrassing tool. She has noticed that Mario isn't hearing well and she wonders whether this is a temporary or permanent condition.

As these thoughts cross Anna's mind, she doesn't notice that the Facebook post is sponsored and that this campaign is targeting women aged 65+ who have an interest in tourism and travel. The Facebook algo knows that Anna has these interests.

Guess how deep the article goes. Anna has an interest in travel and tourism, and the article states clearly, multiple times, that hearing aids from Brand XXX have helped thousands of people in her situation revive their independence. How? By traveling.

Now let's imagine one thing. There is Anna, who has an interest in tourism. However, there is also Jane, who is interested mainly in theater. What if Jane reads a similar article, but this article, instead of talking about tourism, makes clear, repeated references to being able to regularly attend theatre shows?

What if we could build this system for your company? Would you be interested in learning more?

Moreover, do you think that, if one of your competitors is working with us, using similar technology, they would tell you?

Thanks to Facebook's algorithm and our automations we can build a machine that builds an article who speaks directly at your potential patients needs. One wants to hear in order to travel, another one want to hear in order to attend theaters events. They will get stories tailored on them and they will react accordingly to these stories. Accordingly to how well these stories *relate* to them.

Thanks to the digital revolution, we can target every patient at a level that has never before been possible. Your salesperson receives a note from the system and, before even speaking with Anna or Jane, the salesperson already knows their interests, the content they've been fed, and their demographic.

When we worked with our ecommerces and we had famous celebrities wearing our bikinis, we made campaigns with celebrity A targeted towards celebrity A's fans. Shall i tell you how successful these were ?

Thanks to the internet, we can see whether a lead is more susceptible to variables like price depending on how they completed a form, or whether other patients are more susceptible to emotional leverage, such as how big or noticeable the hearing aids are.

All the work that a salesperson would subconsciously do is now done automatically, online, before the patient enters the hearing aid shop. All this is possible now.

HiSmileTeeth

HiSmile is a company that sells tooth-whitening products on the internet. Developed by two talented 22-year-old and 24-year-old entrepreneurs, it had estimated revenue of around $100 million in 2018.

The evolving digital landscape has, over the years, created a demand for <u>better selfies</u>. More millennials are on the internet, uploading and sharing daily photos of themselves.

> Selfie: A **selfie** is a self-portrait type image, typically taken with a smartphone which may be held in the hand or supported by a **selfie** stick

This trend hasn't gone unnoticed by platforms such as Snapchat and Instagram, which offer built-in filters that will make one's skin look smoother or one's teeth whiter.

But that's obviously not enough. HiSmile is not the first tooth whitening product in the world, but it is the first that fought and won to become the most popular among millennials, through digital marketing.

What does this mean, more than being the "Coca-Cola" of tooth whitening brands?

It means that, as this book reiterates, whoever comes first takes all the pie. It doesn't matter if someone invents a better tooth whitening kit in his garage, just as it doesn't matter if somebody invents a tastier version of Coca-Cola. When your product is first in the minds of your customers, you own the entire pie. Now it's too late. You can't have millions of people change their minds that your product will be better.

You could offer more product for a better price (as Pepsi did with Coke) but the point remains the same: Whoever comes first, taking advantage of a new medium, a new channel, takes all the pie.

This applies to HiSmile, to Coca-Cola, to you as a bariatric surgeon, to you as a dentist in any niche or area, and so on. People are working harder in Pepsi's offices than they are in Coke's offices, yet Coke retains most of the pie. Our minds have no place for any other cola brand.

Understanding digital marketing means understanding that our heads don't have room for every product or brand. There is likely no space for your product either, especially if that product is a copy of an existing product. Al Ries and Jack Trout's *"The 22 laws of marketing"* will offer a clear understanding of this positioning concept.

There is a strong, growing desire to look better in pictures (or selfies). Especially in the fashion and cosmetics industries, most products are bought for use in photos. Nowadays people want products that look good in pictures. I have worked for years in fashion and e-commerce, and I believe that there hasn't been another period in history when aesthetics played such a strong role as they do in our society.

Young girls think about breast augmentation in terms of Instagram followers or photo-sharing. Gyms, aesthetic surgeries, cosmetic industries: All these are experiencing increased numbers due to the fact that society is changing.

At the beginning of this book, we said that the elderly are on Facebook while the youth are mainly on Instagram. We took into account Tik Tok (former Musically) and Snapchat, too.

HiSmile is a company that understood how the world is changing and what platforms its audience uses. Acknowledging that your audience is on both Instagram and Facebook, there are two main sources of traffic for HiSmile that we can point out:

1. Testimonials (mainly on Instagram)
2. Paid Ads (on both Instagram and Facebook)

Analyzing what this company did to become first in the minds of their clients, in this new niche, gives us insights that we can utilize for our businesses.

These insights will have a greater impact if we are using the strategies in niches where others before us haven't done the same. Obviously, we can't do what has already been done for years and expect the same results as those achieved by the pioneers of these strategies. However, these insights can be applied to a new, different niche and still produce great results.

I started my career in digital marketing almost ten years ago with Spektre Sunglasses, a Milan-based sunglasses brand that achieved most of its success due to the fact that it had pioneered online product placement strategies. You can now apply these strategies to a brand-new sunglasses project and watch yourself lose millions of dollars.

When we were young, Niccolo Pocchini (Spektre's Sunglasses founder) managed (and still manages) to have his sunglasses in the hands of the most important and influential web personalities. How he did (and does) this is a secret, but only one thing matters to you now: That it worked, and it still works.

Dozens of small sunglass brands arose after Spektre, copying both its style and its communication, but never reached its status. Why? Because they arrived too late.

They would have done better to apply those strategies to…tooth whitening products!

Having a bikini e-commerce brand myself (which is the business that taught us most of what we know), I find the game here to be simple. An internet celebrity has millions of followers. You give her your product. She showcases your product and shares a link so that people can buy it immediately. Boom.

The way we express this strategy here is overly simplistic due to the length of the book and its scope. However, if you're online with a new product (and this also applies to products for patients), a product with real demand, and if you can get famous people to use this product in an authentic way, you're on the path to profit and prosperity.

Please note: Kylie Jenner has one of the most-followed profiles on Instagram. Here she is shown promoting a HiSmile product. Note that she tags @hismileteeth profiles so that users can easily reach and follow the brand's page.

'Tagging' a brand means, inside social networks, to give your follower easy access to the brand's page. This by writing the brand's 'tag' (the same as its virtual address, but inside instagram and facebook) on a post where you're using the product.

Once upon a time products were promoted by celebrities on magazines. Money is flowing more and more from TV, Magazines and billboards to this kind of online digital advertising.

 **HiSmile**
Sponsored · 🌐   •••

Teeth Stains don't have to be forever.
- White Teeth in 10 Minutes
- Up To 8 Shades Whiter
- 100% Money-Back Guarantee ... See More

**WITH A LOYAL
FOLLOWING OF OVER
3 MILLION INCLUDING THE
LIKES OF...**

▶ ●─────────────── -0:21 ⚙ ⛶ 🔇

A retargeting video ad reminds those who already showed interest in HiSmile about its selling points. People can also be re-targeted based on how much of the video above they've seen.

BOOM By Cindy Joseph

Ezra Firestone is a former poker player and one of the most talented internet marketers in the world. Together with Cindy Joseph, he started BOOM, an online beauty cream brand.

Two things set BOOM apart from other brands. The first is its unique positioning. The brand differentiates itself from other cream brands by being Pro-Age.

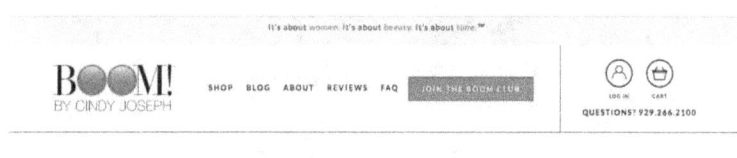

Average creams talk about how to look younger. Meanwhile, BOOM is about embracing the fact that you're aging, and understanding that there is beauty in this.

(Find me a better brand positioning for a new company. While all creams look the same, BOOM has found a way to stand out in a very crowded marketplace!)

The "anti-age" claim implies that something is wrong with the patient/customer. Yet there isn't; aging is natural and happens to all human beings. Ezra and Cindy started from the market, moving the focus away from what all the other brands were doing. This shift is happening in many industries: the "Victoria's Secret" norm of beauty is slowly fading along with its corporate profits and revenues.

The second thing that makes BOOM unique is its internet strategy. Being sold entirely online, the brand has some very sophisticated strategies in terms of both advertising and user experience.

I'll break down the strategy into three pieces, although I could speak about it for months. I chose these three because they are the ones that might best apply to your business.

1. User Experience (how BOOM's website is structured)
2. Community
3. Paid Facebook Advertising

1. User Experience

One's first look at BOOM's website reveals that this is no average e-commerce. In fact, this e-commerce is made to not look like an e-commerce. It looks like a magazine and is much more focused on content than product.

An average anti-age beauty cream e-commerce would have shown a 20-year-old model and made promises about how the client will look miraculously younger thanks to this new blah-blah cream. This would have been shown to the average 60-year-old customer, not taking into account that its competitors were doing exactly the same things, in the same manner. What changes is the ingredient, whether it's "bio" or not, whether some famous testimonial is endorsing it. Not enough!

BOOM makes it clear what it's all about: celebrating women, without unnecessary false promises. BOOM's marketing says, "Hey, this isn't going to create miracles; there are no miracles. But we are women like you and we share the same difficulties: let's be strong together."

The fact that you're not actually pushing products or purchases, but rather are making use of content, causes the user to lower her defenses. Navigation becomes something you do for fun or curiosity, not just to make a purchase. Online shopping is still an activity that many people worldwide regard with anxiety.

One of the most famous BOOM landing pages is this one. Most of the company's ads and traffic direct users to a page like this one (and not a classic product page):

Register   Account   Cart (0)

It's about women. It's about beauty. It's about time.

Call Us (800) 266-6507

BY CINDY JOSEPH

HOME   BLOG   STORE   MODELING   BIO   REVIEWS   PHILOSOPHY   CONTACT   JOIN THE BOOM CLUB

5 Makeup Tips For Older Women By 64 Year Old Makeup Artist Turned Super Model Cindy Joseph!

Cindy Joseph's makeup tips for Boomers

1. **Use cream-based, not powder-based cosmetics on your face.** Powder adds texture to skin that already has developed texture.

2. A good rule of thumb for lipstick is to find a tone that matches the inner lip or gums.

3. **Women older than 50 tend to lose definition in their eyebrows.** Just go with that. Don't recreate the brows you had in your 20s.

4. This is a hard one, but **do not wear any eye shadow at all** (and especially no contour eye shadow in the crease because it gives the appearance of deepening the crease). A little bit of mascara is OK.

5. **Tinted moisturizers don't work.** If you're going to use a foundation to even out skin tone, find one that gives coverage but doesn't add texture. Be willing to spend money on a foundation and take your time to experiment and find the exact right shade. Matching your skin tone exactly is critical.

You can apply this to your online marketing. There is NO reference to your prices, your products, your anything. Here there is only content, information in which your customer is interested. Stop.

Only later, after the potential client has read your content and feels comfortable in your world, can you slowly introduce your product. First we meet, then I sell you something.

BOOM is reportedly earning millions of dollars today.

2. Community

Besides written content, there is no shortage of another form of content on BOOM's website (BOOM is for "Baby Boomers"). That is: testimonials.

The website is full of authentic testimonials. Now, if you're reading this book, you probably already have some patients. While we might not expect you to have built a community or brand, how many of your happy patients does your digital communication showcase? How many video-testimonials do you have?

Building a community around certain values is the surest way to ensure that a flow of money is constantly entering your business. It also helps to hire people who are excited about what you do. (This is better than having people sit there only to collect their salaries.) Money and people are what keep your business alive.

See What People Are Saying About BOOM!

We have a community for my bikini brand, @celest_bikini, and its values are completely different from BOOM's values. We celebrate the right to show off a woman's sexy side without being judged for it. We celebrate the right to undergo plastic surgery if one wants to, and so on.

You see: different niche, different product. Different values and different community. Yet the community behind your brand—both internally (staff) and externally (sales)—is what keeps it alive.

Speaking about the brand on the internet should be actively encouraged. People avidly consume content on the internet before they make even a little purchase. The most trustworthy ones are not celebrities (who can broadcast the message to a wider audience) but normal people—people to whom your customer can relate.

BOOM by Cindy Joseph an honest review

3. Paid Facebook Advertising

When a company, whether in healthcare or not, speaks about itself, it should be very careful in doing so. Nobody really believes a company speaking about itself. The era of "me, me, me" advertising has ended and we had better conserve it for Klondike's liquor ads.

BOOM's advertising team knows that. All their ads are either testimonials or speeches.

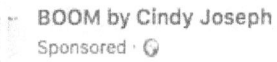 **BOOM by Cindy Joseph**
Sponsored · ⓖ   ···

"All I can say is these little Boomsticks are amazing and easy to use.
They look very natural and I will never use anything else." ~ Sharron W.,
Boomstick Trio customer

These simple, sheer makeup sticks give every woman the look of
happiness, joy and vitality—all with a five-minute application.

Makeup In Minutes

I love the Boom products!

Note the use of quotations, subtitles, and strong visual
effects (lights and a white background). The company

isn't speaking about itself but is having somebody else speak about it.

Most of BOOM's strategies are shared in Ezra Firestone's content. We have given a short introduction to the strategies behind a product aimed at patients. Search "smart marketer" on Google to access more of Ezra's resources.

CHAPTER 9

Other ways you can make a substantial amount of money online

Selling to your colleagues

U p to now, we have regarded online advertising as a tool for acquiring more patients. However, as we market every day to your colleagues, I will tell you something: You can too. The same strategies that this book has put in your hands can be used to ensure that you appear on your colleague's screens in an authoritative way, and remain there for a long time.

In this chapter, we talk about online advertising used for matters that are not directly related to short-term patient acquisition. This can be having people attend an event (any event) or selling courses and offering consulting services to your colleagues.

Online is a great channel for creating public awareness events at which you can show your expertise as a master in your niche, as well as nurture your leads. In that situation, your patients can ask you questions and you can directly answer the public. Needless to say, you can record the meetings for additional online campaigns.

Dr. Joseph A. Gaeta offers some amazing insights into how he could double the number of his implant patients due to his awareness events. I strongly encourage you to search for his work on the internet.

When you organize an event, your first concern should be how to make sure people will attend it. With online advertising, you can attract the attention of the target demographic in your city and have them attend your event. Offering something in exchange (a discount if they accept the treatment, something related to where you are hosting the event) will boost your show-up rate.

While your colleagues are promoting 'free visits', you will have a 30-minute-long video of yourself showcasing your expertise in your niche to a real public. This makes a huge difference. If someone speaks publicly on a matter, any matter, people will perceive them as more authoritative than someone sitting at home.

You might as well be interested in selling your expertise to your colleagues, whether to educate them about scientific disciplines or management ones. They will pay big bucks for that depending on your *reputation*.

Market Research

We use online marketing every day to test projects before heavily investing in them. I have clients who, before they consider opening a new clinic or buying equipment, follow our suggestion of advertising on the internet so that they can grasp the market and the opportunities in the area

I had a client who was going to invest millions in a new cosmetic clinic in a not-so-trendy area. We advised the client to advertise for one month before investing a dime. The client accepted and we found out (after two months of diligent effort) that there was no demand for such services in the area. This suggestion alone made our client millions of dollars. Millions saved.

After a while, another cosmetic clinic opened in the area, and this gave us a tremendous epiphany about the power of digital marketing; the clinic closed after six months. Clearly, nobody in the area was interested in cosmetic surgery.

Mastermind

If you have success in Texas, chances are you can teach others what makes one successful in Nevada without impacting your business. By that, I mean people stealing your "secrets." Chances are, you want to share your expertise and the methods you're using to achieve success now. You'll find that people are willing to pay up to $100,000 for what you can teach them if you're on top of your game.

This kind of money is the sweetest: You work with coachable clients, no hassle, no danger of anything going wrong in an operating room. No equipment costs. No staff to train/organize/hire. Upfront payment.

You'd be surprised about another thing: If you don't promote this, nobody will even think you'd do it. Nobody will care and nobody will pay for it. So you better start recognizing the opportunities you have before someone else catches the fish and leaves you the crumbs. Nobody will be interested in what you can coach them about if there are already 10-20 coaches in your area promoting the same service.

A mastermind or coaching session should be paired with your status and personal branding. The stronger your online presence, the stronger your personal branding, the higher the magnitude of the patients you will acquire, AND the stronger the demand for your expertise.

A continuous and fresh presence online is important for the development of your personal brand. I've seen clients take the same material they use for training their staff and sell it to their colleagues. I mean, sell it for thousands of dollars.

To dozens of people, this means netting $40,000 in one afternoon, which is different from two $20,000 cases. They did not "invent" a new product. They simply took the written procedures they had created for their staff and showcased them to their colleagues.

Surgical Advice

One of the most exciting businesses we're in with surgeons (and with a brand-new company with my partners) is surgical advice. By surgical advice, I mean the process of having a surgeon help a dentist with a difficult case.

Now, let's say there is something you can do but that not all your colleagues can do. You can either teach them (we'll learn about this in the next section) or do it for them. Speaking of high-ticket health treatments, you can do both; they'll learn while they watch you do it (and pay you).

Let's say you're a pioneer specializing in a new solution for your patients.

Now, you can travel at 20 miles per hour and do all the things someone would have done in the 1980s:

Networking, word of mouth, publications, word of mouth, more networking, dinners, events.

Or you can travel at 200 miles per hour and target all your colleagues with your offer.

- Need help with advanced implantology cases? Send us your patient's X-ray plate and get a quote in 24h! -

Advertising on Facebook gives us a pedal. We push on that pedal and we can go as fast as we want. Once you find your way i suggest you to push harder and harder.

Want to grow a business on referral, word of mouth,hope and luck? There's nothing wrong with that but you'll be averaging 20-30 miles per hour. You won't go far.

Want to be known for your accomplishments in your niche? You can build momentum using your name, your ethics, your whatever.

But let's say you want to reach your colleagues now. How do you do that? Let's say you get published by a prestigious magazine in your niche. One hundred of your colleagues read about it.

One hundred is nice, but I'd rather sponsor that article on Facebook and make sure 10,000 colleagues see it. Money follows attention.

You can get a bit of attention on Google. People looking for "dentist" will check your landing page and evaluate, in one or two seconds, whether you're a good pick for whatever service they need.

Or you can create a following, a brand, a name. And not in three decades, but now. Online brands can be created in very little time.

What makes an online brand boring? When it speaks about things that are not relevant to its audience.

When it says the same thing that 100,000 other guys are saying in the same niche.

All these opportunities are golden. However, if you're late, you won't profit from any of them. Opportunities are called this because, as the name suggests, they don't happen often.

Training

Whether technical or managerial, you might have considered teaching something to your colleagues. You don't have to be an 80-year-old expert to teach things to your colleagues. You just need to be one page ahead of them, bring them results, and you're perfectly ok.

Again, every one of us knows something that is worth value. Digital advertising gives us the tools to understand whether there is a real demand for something, even before it is produced.

You'd be amazed that most of the stuff you buy online isn't even produced before you buy it. I'm talking about the books you buy on Amazon. Most of them are printed in Poland before you buy them. You might find it worthwhile to advertise an event before you even rent the place. Top players do it. So should you. Depending on the demand on the internet, you will then rent the room.

You just need a tool that lets you reach thousands of people, and that lets you do it systematically.

The good thing about our work is that we see many, many, many health professionals. We are in contact both with those who are already at the top of their game and with those who are underperforming. This gives us insights into the activities of those who are winning and those who are losing.

Whoever is losing the game doesn't know anything about whoever is winning. Most successful clinics are good at doing just two or three things right. They do them and they succeed. I speak every day with successful health professionals in the seven- to eight-figures realm. They're not geniuses. They are just doing what must be done, and are doing it well. They took advantage of opportunities.

Online advertising is not TV advertising. You can afford it if you're in the six figures with your profession. It works, it makes you money. However, we find it easier to acquire health professionals in the seven figures than health professionals in the six figures. Why? <u>Because health professionals in the seven/eight figures already know that they have to take advantage of opportunities.</u>

They already know they have to do it faster. If you're in the six figures, these guys aren't smarter than you. If we gave an IQ test to you in the six figures and somebody in the seven or eight figures, we'd find that they're not more intelligent than you are. They just do one smart thing that you might not be doing. And they might be avoiding doing 5 to 10 stupid things you're doing. But they probably work the same hours you do. Most of the time even less.

Having access to so many different clinics gives us valuable insight into how things should be done. Today. Not yesterday, not three years ago. The bigger our client base, the more understanding we have of the patient acquisition process.

You probably had problems you solved in your career, and there might be other people stuck in them. These people could be successful, but they have a problem that keeps them stuck.

They can remain stuck on a problem for ages. The wrong team morale can hurt a business to the point that it must close. However, this is a solvable problem. I had this problem and I solved it. You might have it and not even be aware of it.

How do you reach your colleagues who are stuck on something you have already solved? Either you build a brand as a problem-solver offline (not impossible, but people doing that aren't my age, and probably made bigger efforts than I did) or you jump on digital. With digital marketing, you reach them faster.

People doing my job, but with offline methods, ask me, "Hey Max, how do you do that?"

I answer them, "It's not really that we're smarter than you. It's not even that we put in 10 times your effort. It's that we're in a faster car."

The faster car is the internet.

You can run with me on the track and if I'm driving my Porsche GT3 and you're on a Dacia, you can be the best pilot the world ever saw, you can put in 20 times the effort I put in:

But you won't get very far.

When we started this amazing project (Patient-Acquisition.com) , which has been a meteoric success, we started advertising for a clinic that one of my best friends owned.

It was half for fun, half for testing this new idea we had.

And you know what? It wasn't successful. We used too little money, while the copy, the text, the images, everything wasn't good enough.

But again: If you have graduated with a degree in medicine, or if you manage a clinic or a company, you'll probably understand me when I tell you that I'm very, very stubborn.

Even though I was already making money with my other online businesses, at first I thought it was crazy that somebody would have signed up so consistently for dental implantology ONLINE.

But they did, and as of the time of this writing, if you combined all the revenue that my clients have derived from our services, you'd count millions of dollars.

I repeat: millions of dollars a month. And if we keeping doing things right and don't get lost in our journey, we'll soon be producing millions a day.

I was a skeptic too! I would never have believed that this would work if I had not tried it myself.

You might have a solution to your colleague's problem too.

It might be a system, something you teach your employees. It can be the way they answer the phone.

It would be easy to make it into a product and sell it for thousands online. We would be able to show it to the right people. Not the plumber. Not your neighbors. I mean your colleagues.

You can do that too, but reading a book about online advertising alone won't help you. The only thing a book like that can do is give you an epiphany about what is possible today, in your profession, thanks to digital marketing. What you do after that, whom you hire, where you invest, whether or not you invest: It's up to you.

CHAPTER 10

*What all health professionals do wrong
online and what to do about it*

The crowd: A study of the popular mind

T he first deadly sin that most health professionals commit is: not having content. Again, I don't want to repeat myself but: stock photos of patients/doctors a logo designed by your cousin/friend some text about free visits or how much "quality" you offer...

That's not content.

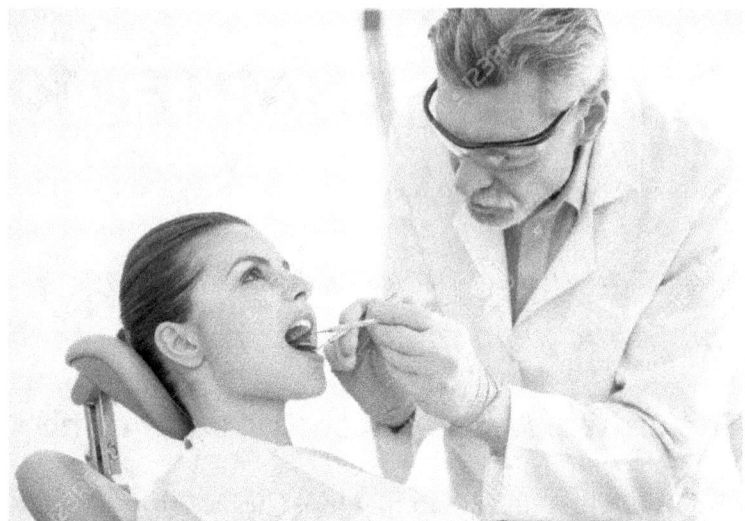

These kind of stock photos <u>are not</u> content

The absence of content means you might have acquired some patients via other offline techniques. However, in 2019 this is as deadly as poison. The elderly are also avid consumers of content. Digital content consumption is growing among all generations to the point where I could see, in the near future, people having their eyes cut out and having a smartphone inserted instead.

This sounds funny but if you realize how the world is going, this will likely be the future. People will be able to consume digital content through contact lenses. Also, it is very likely that we'll have hardware installed directly on our bodies that airs content for us.

Don't worry about that for now BUT you should consider the fact that people are tending to give up TV for the internet. People of all ages are spending hours and hours and hours on their smartphones. They are going to give up everything else to digital content. I know it is not romantic, but that's how society is going, and it is going to affect your life too.

The same 60-year-old man who once regarded Facebook as a waste of time is suddenly an active member in Facebook groups that share their opinions on politics, kittens, coffee, and so on. It's happening everywhere in the world. Fathers and mothers are using Instagram to stalk their daughters; then they end up uploading pictures of the dishes they ordered at restaurants.

Not producing content in 2019 means not having a warm coat when winter is coming. It means summer is almost here and you're out of shape. It means taxes are due but you spent all your money on a car. It's not smart.

We are moving toward a society in which all professionals will need an identity, a brand, content. The world is becoming a huge stage, and we all need to dance, dance, dance. (See more of this in the revolutionary philosophy book by Guy Debord, entitled *La Société du Spectacle*.)

During our careers, we found that the reason why most health professionals don't advertise is not a lack of money (or lack of logic) but fear of what others might think, fear of appearing ridiculous, fear of losing their 'sacred' allure.

Being scared of what others think reminds me of high school, that sense of impotence and inadequacy that I carried with me all the time. It was the reason why I used to smoke, dress a certain way, speak a certain way. All this relates to what I thought people were thinking about me.

Being grown up, I am exposed to criticism every day. I found that all our best, most successful clients are. People insult us for many reasons; they don't like my hair, they don't think health solutions should be advertised, they don't like the way I speak or present myself.

You might find yourself buying cars you don't really need and courting partners you don't really like just to live up to what you want others to think about you. I have been there, you have been there. Having a scope in my life helped me get to the next stage. If you find yourself not creating content because you fear what people might think, because "that's not you," it's time to grow up.

When I started speaking on camera and on stage, and to write controversial things on the state of the health industry in Italy and in the world, it was difficult. I'm an introvert and I could see most people would have made fun of what I was doing. People actually did make fun of me. But you know what? I really believe in what we do here, so we carried on anyway. And you should too.

Not having content doesn't mean I'm suggesting that you act like Kim Kardashian. You don't have to release sex tapes or have a reality crew filming you 24/7. But it means documenting your work. Sharing who you are. It means that when all your patients are asking the same question, you will film a video about it. You'll upload the video. You will post the video again after 6 months.

Yes, it means speaking on video. It means writing. Not writing as if you're writing to the consul of Norway, but writing as if you're writing to a friend about why they should choose this treatment and not that one. And so on.

I'd understand if Osama Bin Laden wasn't uploading his position daily, but if you have a business (a practice IS a business), you're reading this book because you want more patients. If that's the case, you shouldn't act as if you're a terrorist hiding in his Bat-Cave. You should create weekly/daily content.

The more content you create, the more you will be able to show that content to people and the more new patients you will acquire. You will gain more authority when somebody sees the amount of content you produced on that niche.

The quality of your content can boost any patient acquisition campaign tenfold. Quality content does two things: creates emotions and informs.

You might be worried that you will lose your professional status if you advertise but again, it depends on how you advertise, not on the act of advertising itself. We happily advertise health professionals without portraying them as if they're selling fish at the local market.

The point of what we do is not merely to acquire patients, but to have your clinic, your product, your services appear as if they're THE BEST. And I said best, not "very good quality for a low price."

Having content but...

The second deadly sin is producing content but it's too cruent. You might have spent your youth reading books on how the esophagus works. Yet even though you're probably a smart person, you end up using

The same images

The same language

in your content. That isn't the language you use with your patients when you speak one on one (I hope) and it's not something anybody except a surgeon wants to see.

Why do 99 percent of doctors share stuff that looks like university research? Your patients don't want to see that stuff. If you miss university and you want to return, then go and create content for your colleagues. If you want to fish, you need to think like a fish. Fishes don't want to see that stuff.

Trucid content

Surgeons: We need to find a way to show your content while minimizing the presence of syringes, blood, and human meat. I know that this stuff doesn't faze you. You see it all the time. If you're a surgeon, you're probably not shocked when you see blood or syringes.

You use syringes all day for filler punctures and the patient is happy. Yet the potential patient might not be. I know that a patient who has already had her third non-surgical rhinoplasty probably won't care about syringes. But a potential patient might.

I like to think that you're a fairy with a magic wand. You do fillers: you do injections. But does anybody really want injections? If people loved injections, there would be queues in front of the blood donation office.

Do your patients want bigger lips? Why don't we show them bigger lips and minimize the presence of syringes?

<u>The product and the process are not as important as the outcome.</u> People want holes in walls, not drills.

It's the same for dental implantology, etc. You don't want your page to look like it belongs to a butcher. And while what I say here seems obvious, review your content and then get back to this book. If you have content, it's highly likely you've committed this sin.

In trichology, I see the same thing. It's not as invasive but any trichologist's content still manages to look pretty trucid. You're selling hair, sex, confidence, not holes in the patient's head.

If we're removing tattoos, can we please speak about how the patient is starting a new era in their life, how they're getting rid of the past? We don't need to see reddish marks on someone's arm.

Before-and-after photos

You probably studied medicine, or at least management. I understand you might not have the tools to understand this and I'd probably be in your situation if my libraries were full of vasectomy books instead of marketing ones.

However, most before-and-after photos I see are very trucid and bad-looking. Let's look at yours.

(P.S. Having bad-looking before-and-after photos is better than having no content at all.)

Let's look at your before-and-after pictures. Do you shoot them with a black background? I know it might be easier to shoot like this, but:

- It doesn't look pretty.
- Have you noticed? Everyone else is doing it.

This means that your competitors are probably doing the same thing. If your competitors are sleeping and not producing content, that just means that sooner or later somebody else will be doing it...and they're going to look make it good.

However, you don't want to be chosen based solely on your before-and-after photos. You build a brand around yourself, you build stories. You want to be chosen because of what you represent, because of your reputation. People must choose you for your name, for the names of the people you've worked with, for the experience you'll give them, for the status they'll get when they choose you. Whether they've been smart in choosing you, whether they'll be part of an elite group, whether they'll have an interesting story to tell about you.

If your work comes down to simply checking who looks best in before-and-after photos, you (or your competitors) are not doing marketing right. Plus, your patients don't have the means to really differentiate good work from average work either!

I know you'd prefer a job in which aesthetics and image don't matter this much but the drive that is pushing you to create content and promote it online is the same drive that, most of the time, is filling your agenda. You can try to stop this energy that is bringing you more and more online, but that would be like fighting a dam's overflow.

You can't expect to acquire patients based on how valuable you are on the inside if your outside appearance is LAME.

I wish girls would love me for my kindness but this doesn't seem to work. Appearances count. More than before. And tomorrow they will count more than they do today. You can embrace it, adapt to it, or just go down the road and protest how far we've gone. There are no "real" things; there are only appearances.

Before-and-after pictures are such a strong visual selling point that Facebook prohibits their promotion. You can post them organically on your Instagram and Facebook feeds, but if we promote them (paid promotion), it is very likely that your ad account would be shut down. Not a good thing.

So we have to be smart about them. And honestly, I understand why Facebook doesn't want its feed filled with before-and-after photos.

When you do before-and-after photos, make sure you are not portraying only the body part. Show the full person. Show the story. I know the patient wants to see the body part, but, if you can, show the whole human being. The human being has a story. <u>You relate to human beings; you don't really relate to body parts.</u> Show readers that it's real. Then show them the details of your job, but only if the patient actually wants to see them (clicking, sliding the photos).

Invest in your material. Don't buy a $1,000 camera (you might not really need it) for photos you can shoot with an iPhone X. Invest in lights, a green board (later adding what you want), a white carpet, flash, filling light. You can buy these items on Amazon for $100. I also like those round lights with a hole in between for securing the camera/iPhone. They work well and I myself look good with them.

Tip: the camera is not as important as the light. Invest in lights before than everything else

Blacking out patients' eyes is very, very ugly. I understand that all your patients might not want to appear on camera, but trust me when I tell you that the most successful surgeons I know (like Giacomo Urtis, which i really admire and i urge you to check on @giacomourtis page on Instagram) don't censor their patients' faces. <u>Uncensored content works simply better than censored content</u>. The only reason you use censorship is that you believe your patients don't want to be on your Instagram feed. That might not be as true as you think.

You can help yourself using Photoshop, too. Don't create things you didn't actually do. However, if your patient comes in for the "after" photo and her skin isn't looking good that day for whatever reason, you'll want to edit it with some filter. Read again: I'm not saying to edit the work you did during the actual operation, but making the surroundings look better can be a good idea.

It seems that most health professionals' worst nightmare is being robbed of their cases photographs. So, depending on their taste, they apply a badge to every photo.

First: Relax

Second: The badge, if you want to use it, must be small. Otherwise, it will look spammy and make the picture look bad. Again, I know everybody does it, and I know that if you don't do it you'll find a surgeon in India pretending your patients are theirs. But you can't do what everybody else in your niche is doing and expect extraordinary results. Extraordinary results follow extraordinary actions. Unique actions.

Do some math. How many patients can you acquire if your photos are clean and nice and how many patients will you actually lose if somebody steals those photos?

P.S. People can remove your watermarks using Photoshop anyways

Now, let's say you have hundreds of beautiful before-and-after photos. As I told you, we can't promote them. But wait: We can't promote them directly. We can still drive people to your Instagram page, where they'll then see the photos. If you know and respect the rules, you can always find a way.

Lights and background

Most sanitary premises have very cold lighting and the person who takes the photos doesn't have a clear understanding of color and light. Take a look at the most famous influencers on Instagram or Facebook, the most successful e-commerces. You'll learn something.

Whether they're a fashion blogger or a surgeon, they are successful on the web due to the quality of their content. Followers on Instagram aren't numbers: they're real people who want to be entertained.

And yes: Lights and background matter. A lot.

<u>Adding an "inspiration" photo to your before-and-after is a wonderful idea</u>. You can place a famous Instagram star there. So, you'll have a "before" photo, and "after" photo, and an "inspiration" photo. This will immediately drag your patient's mind to that star's status/content. I first saw Dr. Lara Devgan doing this on her profile and I must compliment her.

Not telling stories

Showcasing human body parts on the internet is better than showing nothing at all. However, it still sucks. You should tell a story with every case, and every story should be rich in details to which any target patient can relate.

You should already grasp the 8-10 most common objections you get when you present treatments. Your stories should address these objections.

Again, with online marketing, we address these objections BEFORE we actually see the patient. The patient should already be sold before the two of you meet. This is the role of content. This is the role of stories. It's why we tell them.

Jesus Christ told stories to influence people. This "story" stuff is HUGE. If you have only before-and-after photos, you'd better level up. Like Jesus. Reflect for a second on how far these stories have gone, how many times they've been retold, the incredible effects they've had on the world.

The internet is the best place to tell stories today. We don't have records of before-and-after narrations of the Bible. The bible hasn't reached everybody in the Western world like this. "Lazarus was dead, then Jesus came and he lived." This isn't how you should tell the story.

Nobody will remember your before-and-after pictures for long. But people will remember your stories. Who you represented, what you stood for. <u>Don't be a technician in your work, be a story-teller</u>. I've never met a rich technician who was just a technician.

In the end, these are just stories. Good stories. Good content. Some of them might actually never have happened but hey: People want to listen to and believe in stories. They are going to remember these stories for how they made them feel.

Make your story as detailed as possible and make sure you have as many stories as you have groups of patients. You should already have an idea of the different groups of patients you have. You can divide them in terms of demographics, salary, cultural backgrounds, values, etc. People are getting breast augmentations because they're in the fourth pregnancy and people are getting breast augmentations because they're going to college. People are getting breast augmentations because they're transitioning from male to female. Remember to speak to all of them, depending on your positioning. The all of them need a different story.

Your positioning is who you are in your niche. Are you the person who does breast augmentation for those undergoing sex transitioning, or for those who want to be Instagram Famous? Different patients, different messages. If you want to take everybody, know that you can but only if you're the first in your category. If somebody else is already top in your category you have to choose a sub-category.

I'll tell you a story about this. You are probably uncertain about specializing in a tight niche such as breast augmentation for those undergoing a sex transition, especially if you're in a small city. This story relates to many aspects of human psychology.

When I was younger I was very into understanding how young girls picked boys. I saw things I could not understand. How did very ugly guys still get pretty girls? And no, it wasn't because of money or anything else. There's no space for banality here. I'm talking about a real study. It is common to see some sort of disproportion among couples, and whereas now i don't care, at the time the thing puzzled me.

Pay attention, i'll use an example :

Let's say we are looking for someone to use Photoshop for one of my bikini companies. We are looking for freelancers on the web. I could go for the one who has the most reviews (say, if it was a man, it was the most popular or the prettiest). Or, if I had a particular need (not generic Photoshop, or Photoshop for bikini shoots) I might find somebody with much fewer ratings but who specializes in editing ONLY bikini shots on Photoshop.

Who would any reasonable one choose? We—and you—would go for the one who specializes in bikinis, even if they have three reviews rating them four stars out of five. And we'd forget the company that has 334 five-star-reviews.

Why? Because we're looking for bikini freelancers. We have a specific need and we'll be magnetized by who better relates to it. Not the most famous freelancer. Not the cheapest or the most expensive. Not the one with best reviews. But the one who better relates to our needs.

The same thing happens with dating. Women evaluate the commonalities among men. They study them. All girls, after their firsts relationship, develop a "kind" of guy, depending perhaps on physical characteristics or even a trait they're unaware of.

<u>Most health professionals try to do everything. However, some of the most successful ones are doing just one thing very well.</u> We could be doing digital advertising for lawyers and health professionals, but we would be

weakening our message. Thats why we work solely on acquiring patients. We don't work with lawyers.

Your stories should reflect who you are. And who you are professionally is something you should decide beforehand, if you haven't yet done so. It doesn't really matter what you choose, but by focusing on one thing (so long as it's not too narrow), you will be able to create a name for yourself more easily.

If you do generic breast augmentations for everybody, you can still put food on your table but you can't break out as a star in what you do, as there will be no evidence indicating that someone should choose you.

Looking like a salesperson

I'll be short here. You should always look calm on camera. I myself can get excited while explaining new opportunities in online marketing, but you can't. The marketing strategies I use, or that some of my colleagues use, are not for necessarily for you. Marketing for salespeople or car dealers IS NOT marketing for the health industry. Please make sure you don't look like you're selling cars or pitching start-ups. You're speaking to patients: not investors, not car buyers.

A doctor should always look calm and should never be pushy. A patient can be anxious, but a doctor can't.

A doctor is like a steward on your Maldives trip. You don't want to see them crying or yelling. Ever.

You're an expert. Act like an expert.

I recommend that you not include price in your online campaigns unless that's your only strong selling point. And if price is the only selling point you have in health, we probably don't want to work with you.

Not showing lifestyle

Make sure your lifestyle matches your values and your ideal patient base. You should not only hang out in places where you can find dozens of patients but you should showcase this lifestyle.

You're an expert, right, but to make your personal branding stand out, to create a connection with your patients, you must show them a bit of who you are, what you do, your values, your luxuries.

If you're selling to the affluent, you don't want to look cheap. If you're doing an event, show it. If you're studying a complicated matter related to your patients, show it.

I assume you want to stand out and attract high-income patients, so I suggest that you regularly get yourself photographed with celebrities. As much as you can. It doesn't matter whether they're your patients, because you just want your patients to associate them with you.

And that association comes subconsciously so that they can't stop it from happening, even if they want to.

Your lifestyle when you're not working is part of who you are; it's part of your personal branding.

You need your patient to dream about being you. They're not going to choose you only for what you do, but mostly for who you are.

Not being a celebrity

You might whine all day about "Why I'm not making enough money" or "Why aren't they coming to my door?" I understand that not everyone has the drive to become a celebrity. However, I must tell you that all the health professionals who are doing better than you are…are more famous than you are.

Bizarre, right? But that's how it is. Today your biggest threat comes from people in your niche who are advertising more than you are, who are reaching more people than you are, and who are reaching those people more often. They are the guys who are stealing your patients.

If, when you post on Facebook, you reach 32 people, your competitors might post something uglier and not as effective, but they are reaching 32,000 people...and yes, they are taking attention away from you. You end up acquiring patients just because they're friends of friends of friends and you give good deals to friends. But friends are for leisure; business is another thing entirely.

CHAPTER 11

Understanding patients' psychology: What makes the patient's mind tick?

On the fallacy of patients' stream of consciousness

You might have realized: When it's a matter of deciding what is best for their own health, patients don't choose well. You see this every day in your niche. If you're a bariatric surgeon, you'll see obese patients buying into detox tea. If you're a dentist, you'll see people choosing low-cost chains and getting dental implants that will last two to 5 years. If you're a cosmetic surgeon, you'll see patients whom your colleagues and competitors have messed up. Patients don't choose well. However, I want to tell you something else: When it comes to marketing, 99.9 percent of health professionals don't choose well either.

This is why marketing is important. If you were able to fill your clinic simply by being good at what you do, you'd be living in a fairy tale. Doing your job right isn't enough. The sad truth is that you will find people doing a worse job than you are but earning 100 times more.

This is why we need marketing. It's time for you to realize that every problem you have is a marketing problem. Not just the problems you have with your clinic, with your business, but also the problems you have in your personal life, in your relationships. All these problems come down to the perception people have of you. Marketing is the management of those perceptions.

When you have power over those perceptions, you are doing well. When those perceptions are bad, you're not doing well. This book is different from other digital marketing books because:

I haven't taught you what 'Instagram Stories' are.

I haven't taught you about YouTube marketing.

Or SEO.

Or the complicated details of Facebook ads.

Why? For two reasons. The first is that you don't need them. You're not a media buyer. People on my team need this kind of information. You don't.

The second reason is that teaching you what Snapchat is will not make you better, and will not help you understand what is best for you. If you don't know what Snapchat is, search on Google.

Regarding deontological issues: You might have found that it doesn't matter how much you genuinely love your patients; you could be breaking even, sacrificing your margins for charity, and still have problems acquiring patients.

There is no correlation between your deontological values and the number of patients you are able to acquire. You can be the sweetest, most honest doctor or hospital manager on the planet; still, there is no actual correlation between that and the number of patients you can acquire and treat.

The fact that you're broke doesn't mean you are more ethical than your competitors (although I've seen many broke health professionals who believe this). The fact that somebody is earning 100 times what you are and is a celebrity in their profession does not mean they are unethical or are committing crimes. They are just better at acquiring patients than you are. Accept it.

Your patients' mental processes related to decisions are flawed. To do the best, in their best interest, you need to understand what makes their minds tick. They have to choose better and they won't be able to do so if you keep your arms crossed, thinking about how ethical you are. It's not an ethics matter. Whoever takes advantage of these leverages, today, thanks to the internet, can profit. If you believe there is value in what you provide, and if you believe you can provide more value than your competitors can, it is an obvious consequence that you will want to acquire as many patients as possible. You will do good for both you and them.

What makes a patient's mind tick: Information

The need for information is often underrated. So is the quantity and quality of information.

I forecast that in every area, in every corner of the world, those health professionals who become the first sources of information for their niche, providing fresh and constant information, will take it all.

If that person is you, you will acquire all your competitors' patients. If that person is your competitor, well…you know what will happen. You'll end up with fewer patients every year, and after a while you'll end up copying your competitors' strategies. However, you will be copying them too late, and without a vision. And copying is never good. You should be first.

You know what causes big malls to close in the US (and all over the world)? For electronics, it's the fact that now a price is readily available everywhere. You can find an iPhone at a lower price. Consumers know it. The consumer is not a moron down the street; the consumer is your wife. She knows where to shop.

Information is becoming easily available to everyone. To your patients, too.

This means that the figure of the doctor knowing it all, in his little town, prescribing treatments depending on his own will, is GONE FOREVER.

Ten years ago, there weren't many forums where people shared their experiences with a treatment. Now there are. Everybody checks for that before considering a treatment. People search for symptoms online BEFORE they ask their doctors. This is a tremendous force that is reshaping your profession. You can either take advantage of it or be defeated by it.

In the past, a health professional had more power due to the slow circulation of information among patients. This is changing fast, and it will change your life.

Moreover, because you can't ask for a sale on every piece of content you produce, most of it must be pure information.

People genuinely want to learn. Even if it's not their treatment, you will see that they are fascinated by what you have to tell them.

Again: This kind of work must be a vocation for you. It is not something you do 3 times and then give up because you got only 2 likes on each Facebook post. (Hint: Facebook posts without promotion are not the places to do this.)

You can't do it 2 or 3 times and then give up, because somebody will show up and do it 200 or 300 times. And this person will take it all. Your patients will deny your treatment options because they have read your competitors' content, which was not quite aligned with yours.

Most of the time, information on the Internet isn't correct. However, if it is easily available, it is *assumed* to be correct. Not in the real world, but in your patients' minds—which are the only minds you should care about.

I know that in the 1980s, 1990s, and 2000s you could make millions using other strategies, in other ways. But this is how things work today and how they'll work tomorrow. So you'd better listen to it and stick to it. Or you could still use the strategies of the 2000s in the 2010s and 2020s.

Or better yet, you could have no strategy at all.

Needless to say, all successful people have a strategy. That might be something they did not teach you at medical school (and relax: probably not at business school either), but it is something any successful health professional can tell you. Every successful health professional has a clear strategy, and when you can't fully evaluate one, you need somebody to help you with that.

What is your strategy? Is your strategy to actively broadcast information on a large scale, through the internet, to spread that information?

Is it to have better-informed patients so that you can sell them on the fact that you're an authority in the matter?

Your patients don't want to research for ages. They want certainties. They'll choose you because you're the only one giving certainties to them. They'll stop wasting their energy thinking about their treatment: they'll just believe you, no matter what. People are lazy. Once they accept your role, it's done. That is why you should invest over half your time, your energy, your income in this before you invest in medical equipment.

The process in which there was a doctor, in his little town, having that authority, has changed. Now there is no town, even if you're in a small town. With the internet, people have access to all the information they need. Even though they don't want to search, they will if they're obliged to do so.

The need for information is often misunderstood. I'll tell you a story about this. Let's say I'm with my girlfriend and she wants to get a breast augmentation. We go to see two surgeons in Milan.

One of them speaks to us for 25 minutes and then has to go. The other one takes an hour, lets her try on the prosthesis (there are shirts made for that), talks about the price, describes the advancement of the technology, discusses the risks, answers all her questions, and comes up with more questions.

Which would you choose? Now, I know what you're thinking...

- *I can't take one hour for every potential patient; not all of them accept! I'll spend my days and weeks simply prospecting! -*

You are right! This is why you need an online system that automatically sends this information to your potential leads BEFORE you meet them. You don't have to repeat this process 1,000 times. You'll just do it once and we'll automate it so that 1,000 potential patients (hot leads) will see it.

Again, you know the story of Encarta, right? In the 1980s, encyclopedias were sold door to door, and you could buy a set for $1,500-$2,000.

Good deal, right? Everyone was happy. The biggest companies were close to grossing half a billion dollars in encyclopedias

What nobody foresaw was that Microsoft was developing a virtual encyclopedia that IMMEDIATELY destroyed the paper encyclopedia business. That was Encarta.

I had both encyclopedias and Encarta in my home. Now when I need information, I put an Encarta CD in my desktop compact disk reader and I have all the information I need!

Obviously, I'm joking. Nobody on earth does that anymore. We all look on Wikipedia, right?

This story is for you to ask yourself: Are you an encyclopedia, Encarta, or Wikipedia?

Because, yes, these changes are affecting your life too. Not as a consumer but as a professional.

It all comes down to the decision you make when you close this book. It doesn't really matter if you agree with what I say; if you don't take action when you close this book, or with this book open, you will still be Encarta.

My laptop doesn't even have a CD reader anymore, by the way.

What makes a patient's mind tick: Price

Price should not be your main selling point. If you have the lowest prices, I'm not sure we want to work together. Here, we're in health; we're not talking cheeseburgers or hardware imported from China.

I don't personally advise showcasing prices or promotions as the first selling point in your communication. Having said that, price is one of the most important leverages in your patients' minds.

While you want to eliminate potential patients who want to know only the price (just to do comparison shopping), you must understand their psychology. You must reach and nurture this potential patient. You must do this in an automated way so that your marketing will knock at their door day after day after day. You just automate it and then forget about it.

With our patient acquisition strategies, we acquire patients in the short term. This means you'll treat them this week and then the next. However, thinking that the results are just there would be reductive. A patient might wait 1-2 years before they have the courage to go for a major, high-ticket treatment. They'll go with you if you've nurtured them along the way. They will see the continuity of your content and they will feel safe.

You must produce content that warns patients to not be attracted by cheap prices. In your communication, you want prospective patients to know about the risks they're taking on when they're treated at the lowest prices.

You must also accept that you're not going to be a good fit for every patient. Not everybody will be able to afford your services. The sooner you understand this, the better off you'll be.

What makes a patient's mind tick: Authority

How authoritative are you in your niche? Here comes the focus point we talked about in the previous chapters. If you're focused on all kinds of cosmetic surgery and you meet a patient interested in breast augmentation, you will have less authority than your colleague who focuses only on breast augmentation. (We're taking for granted that you are perceived as the same on all other matters.)

It's up to you whether you present yourself as the Michelangelo (or Picasso) of breast augmentation. The deeper the focus on a specific matter, the more your authority grows. You don't want to focus on a smaller niche, but being too generic won't help you, either. You can't do everything.

What makes a patient's mind tick: Celebrity

People love celebrities and your being associated with them will change your professional life. The more famous the celebrities you hang out with, the higher the prices you can charge. Full stop.

Patients have flawed perceptions of your value as a health professional, and this example is the strongest evidence of that. Like it or not, this is how the human mind works. You'd better take advantage of it or risk having your competitors steal your high-ticket patients.

Having you seen treating celebrities is a risky task, as there are no official "prices." I know this myself, as some of the most famous celebrities in the world wear both Celest Bikinis and Meow Bikinis. You'll want to be helped by somebody who has experience in the matter.

What makes a patient's mind tick: Empathy

The magic that happens when you speak one on one. When they ask you questions as if you were the only trustworthy expert in the world.

This isn't something you're born with. This is something you develop by working on yourself and seeking help from a professional. Most super-professionals we know have had coaches help them present prices and treatments.

We reached the point of recording our clients' front-office calls to identify flaws that might have caused the practice to underperform economically. On this matter, we could write another book, so I'll leave that topic for the next one.

What makes a patient's mind tick: Emotions

Lastly, what makes the patient's mind tick isn't your authority, your face, the information you give them. They will use emotions to determine whether they'll accept your treatment.

I recommend that you, as a health professional, *suggest* an emotion-related reason but not be pushy. Always remember, though, that in the end, your patients will make the move due to emotions and not rationality.

If you can spark an emotion, write a story in your patient's mind (maybe the story of one of your other, happy patients, someone with a similar and relatable background?), they'll make the move.

I know this from personal experience. As of the time of this writing, I had undergone a surgical treatment a week ago. I had delayed it for weeks, months (and maybe 2 years if I'm being fully honest).

I had the money, I had faith in the surgeon, I had the time. But I postponed it twice. What was missing was the emotional push that led me to bring myself to the clinic. Don't underestimate the fact that nobody really likes surgery except for the experienced and passionate surgeon (working on somebody else's body).

An automated machine that addressed my objections would have brought me there two years earlier. A few emails and some content would have built up my courage to act immediately, because people ultimately choose based on an emotion that content has sparked.

Let's say you warn your patients about something. Doing so once within your clinic walls might not have a long-lasting effect. Exposing them to daily or weekly content about *the risks of not acting now* would have a stronger impact. This is exactly the revolution I'm talking about. The revolution that is changing the way you work, forever.

Healthcare professionals will be able to track who faces the risk of a heart attack *before* the person actually suffers from one. They will be able to broadcast content that persuades the individual to accept a treatment *before* it's too late.

You will be able to treat and see your patients from another city while sitting in your home…through the internet. Devices are coming out now that can track your patients' heart rate directly from their smartphones. This is happening today; it's not some strange revolution that will happen in 10 years. Today, hospitals are offering medical examinations through the internet.

Who is going to take advantage of this revolution, of these immense opportunities today? The ones who will benefit the most from them. The ones who will see their careers and lives take completely new turns.

CHAPTER 12

Two offline actions that will cause your online results to skyrocket

Shock-and-awe kit and Front Desk phone scripts

Although I strongly advise that you use digital as the only opportunity for doubling your revenue, and I advise that you do it now (because the later you jump into the boat, the worse your result will be), ultimately you're not an e-commerce.

What I mean by this is that you are not selling goods online. You're a physical, real business. Digital marketing is a means of attracting the attention of potential patients, having them raise their hands and say, "Hey! Here I am!"

After that moment, the funnel continues, but it continues *offline*. What happens when your front office calls them, what happens when you present them with a quote face to face: all these things are equally important and you must have them under control if you want online to work.

Online can't work if your front office staff chews gum while on the phone with your potential patients and doesn't call a lead more than once if they don't answer on the first attempt.

The two offline strategies I'm disclosing now will cause your online results to skyrocket. They both refer to what happens *after* a lead has been acquired online.

Shock-and-awe kit

Marketing legend Dan Kennedy is the inventor of the "Shock and awe kit". This powerful selling tool can be used in any industry: especially Healthcare

The concept behind a shock-and-awe package is to create a benefit-laden kit that is so unique-looking and full of useful content, the recipient has no other choice but to notice it and choose you as their go-to solution.

Now, let's assume you work with my agency and we are sending you 20 high-ticket treatment patients every week. You either receive these people's contact information or they contact you directly. These people have been fed your unique content and are highly interested in being treated by you. These are not people looking for "Dentist New York"; these are people who have a problem in your niche, who have read all your selected material, who already know about you and the unique way you can solve their problems.

However, as with dental implants, we work with treatments averaging $30,000 each; there might be a large gap between words and deeds. Expecting to have all 20 high-ticket patients accept the price quotation NOW would be excessively optimistic.

The idea behind a shock-and-awe kit, sent directly to someone who has just booked an appointment with your clinic for a high-ticket treatment, is to invade their space, both physically and mentally.

Let's assume they are not ready to accept the quote for whatever reason. If they received books about you, a toothbrush with your name on it, a dozen testimonials in booklets and brochures, DVDs, guarantees, who else would they possibly choose?

It might take them 6 months, 12 months, but if you invaded their space first and nobody has yet used this strategy with them, how much better will their perception of you be in comparison to their perception of one of your competitors? A shock-and-awe kit is the strongest sales content you can possibly have, all wrapped up to look like a gift to your potential patient.

Let's say you have a patient telling you, "Hey, I am highly interested in this bariatric treatment because I'm obese," etc.

If you follow this book's suggestions, you'll:

- Book an appointment with her.
- Send her retargeted ads, on multiple platforms, so that you'll be on her mind.
- Send her a list of emails to remind her that what's right for her health should be done NOW.
- Have her speak on the phone with a trained professional from your front office who will follow a script you've developed covering all objections, side effects, and benefits. The focus will be on attaining information and having the patient book the appointment.
- Send her a shock-and-awe kit that invades her space. The kit will showcase stories of women

you treated successfully and to whom she can relate.

- Have her visit your office and, finally, speak to her one on one, seeking to get her to accept the treatment.
- Record her transformation story so that you can use it as a referral for your marketing automation.

When I say that, with our strategies, we have had health structures double or triple their topline revenue, people might not believe me immediately. Yet after having read this book, you should grasp what is possible if you act now. This stuff works and can make you rich. It changes my clients' lives day after day

Not only does it make you richer but it makes you more famous and authoritative. It makes your patients happier. It makes your family prouder of you and it helps your patient's family relax, knowing their loved one is in the hands of a real professional.

Now let's dive into the benefits of a shock-and-awe kit:

- Low unit price. You won't have to spend more than $10-$15 for each, shipping included.
- High perceived value. Your competitors aren't doing this (and if they are, your shock-and-awe kit should look better than theirs!).
- Patients receive answers to their questions BEFORE they see you. They can check these

answers any time they want, in the quiet of their own home.

- You have them pay for a visit after you send them this. No more free visits!
- Reciprocity: You gave them a present, so now they feel like they owe you something.
- Higher referral rate: This physical content is easily shared and becomes an object of discussion when friends with a similar problem visit your patient's home. For this reason, we usually include multiple booklets in the kit.
- Invasion of space: Your patients will see your name every day. (This is the point of the gifts you send them.)
- The patient regards you as more trustworthy and as an authority.
- The patient will more likely accept your quote without objections.

Now let's look at what's inside one of our average shock-and-awe kits:

A customized letter to the patient; the more details about them, the better.

Physical gifts: Yogurt, toothbrushes, toothpaste, detox stuff, etc., each with your logo or name printed on it.

A testimonial book or booklet, with your happy stories and a short narration. This is one of the most important parts of your kit.

A warranty!

Informative booklets about the treatment: the risks, the procedure, how to prepare for it, etc.

Business cards.

A nice-looking cardboard box.

After the patient receives the kit, one of your front office representatives should call her and make sure she will show up for the visit: "Hey, I just wanted to make sure you received our shock-and-awe kit!"

On average, the use of a shock-and-awe kit doubles the conversion rate of one of our online campaigns. This is the strongest sales asset you'll have. It's better than investing in SEO and offering free visits, right?

Front Desk Phone Scripts

DDS Simone Stori is with his Dental SPA (Bologna, Italy) on top of dental procedures management. Some of the scripts tactics we illustrate here have been developed by him and his team and shared on one of his private mastermind events.

Imagine if you could receive, every day, 10 calls from potential patients, with your front office capable to convert 50% of such calls in first appointments.

Now imagine that, after reading these paragraphs, you show this material to your team and you put your efforts in the systematisation of the appointment acquisition process of your clinic (also by registering all the calls).

Let's make the assumption that this material you are reading will bring you even just <u>1 new appointment</u> scheduled for every day.

It would amount in 20 appointments every month.

240 appointments for the year.

How worth are for you 240 appointments in one year?

This chapter alone can change the future of your practice: don't just read this, apply it!

There is no instrument more delicate than the phone, for a practice oriented to customer care or marketing.Offer to every potential patient, during the phone call, a pleasant experience, ignite the "wow effect" for her or for him, and it will be much easier to land a new appointment for her/him or a member of the family. Treat them poorly, without care or without a smile...and they will not schedule the appointment, and maybe even say bad things about you!

P.s. the script is not something that should be read and recited as it is over the phone, but rather a guideline to follow and to have available during the phone call

SMILE! It's the first trick for a successful call.

Even though no one can see us from the other side of the call, a phone call should always start with a big smile on our face, continue and end without the smile leaving our face.

SO, RULE NUMBER 1:

Put on your best smile and...start with energy!
Your energy and your positivity are extremely important, as your whole approach to the phone call.

2: ANSWER BEFORE THE THIRD RING

When a potential or actual patient calls, a nice behaviour rule is to avoid multiple selection call center, and always try to answer before the third ring.

3: PRONOUNCE THE NAME OF THE PATIENT AT LEAST 3 TIMES

There is nothing more sweet and persuasive for a person than the sound her/his name. Always ask for the name and try to use it at least 3 times during the course of the phone call.

4: 100% FOCUSED

We all know the acceptance desk of a dental clinic may be one busy place! But when you make phone calls, you should always be 100% focused on that phone call. If you are distracted or not enough focused, the person on the line will know right away.

5: TONE OF VOICE AND LANGUAGE

During the calls you should keep a medium-high voice tone, articulate your words and talk calmly. Even better, you should try to adjust the words, the tone and the speed of your voice with the person on the line, to get in sync with her/him.

6: DO NOT EAT OR USE CHEWING GUMS

It is fundamental, when you work on the phone, to avoid eating or using chewing gums. The person you are talking to will likely notice it, and it will disturb significantly the phone call.

7: DO NOT PUT ON HOLD

A common situation, especially in the less organised clinics, is receiving a phone call while the employee at the desk is serving a patient.

Here is the correct way to handle the situation:

1. Ask permission to answer the call to the patient being served.
2. Answer in a calm and appropriate way.
3. Tell the person on the line: "Thank you for calling, [HER/HIS NAME]. May I put you on hold for one moment, or may I call you back, as I am serving a patient right now? So that I can be at your full disposal. What would you prefer?"
4. If on hold, thank the person and put on hold. Let them know if the waiting time exceeds 2 - 3 minutes.
5. If call back, ask again the phone number to call at, for confirmation.
6. Thank her/him heartedly.

8: GET THE PERSON INVOLVED AND CONTROL THE PACE

It is fundamental to empathise with the person right away, and emotionally involve her/him. Let's make an example. If a person calls, asking "I need a root canal therapy. How much does it cost?", it is possible to elaborate on the subject, for example by asking:

- Why are you asking for a root canal therapy?
- Does it hurt when it's hot or cold? Or while eating?
- How long has it been hurting?
- As you hear the person's answers, show yourself interested and try to get in sync with her/him. A really key question in urgent requests management is the following: "When can you come here?". If the matter is really urgent, the only answer really is "Now"

9: ESTABLISH AUTHORITY

During the call, the staff member at the front desk becomes the authority. The patient, actual or potential, relies on her/his advice. It becomes therefore important to teach the staff to sing the praises of the clinic and of the doctor. An example could be:

> "You know, for periodontitis issues you really have called at the right place! Doctor [NAME] is really experienced in the field and has treated countless patients with the same problem! You will find yourself very happy, and you will find the best solution for your budget and your needs!"

10: OFFER AN APPOINTMENT

<u>The only objective and result that is allowed is to schedule an appointment.</u> (But also to avoid patients that are significantly off your ideal target of patient)

Once you have acquired familiarity with the potential patient, and identified her/his needs, don't simply ask "Would you like to schedule an appointment?", but, instead, go ahead and offer directly a couple of options (better if one is in the morning and the other in the afternoon), for example:

"It looks like you need to see the doctor as soon as possible. Would you rather monday at 11.00 am or Tuesday, 4.00 pm?"

This way, you are assuming that the caller has already decided to schedule an appointment.

11: ALWAYS RECAP AND TAKE NOTE OF ALL INFORMATION

As you proceed towards the end of the call, there is a fundamental step before hanging up the phone, which is to <u>make a recap of the call.</u> In particular, when possible, go over the caller's problem again, how the caller is feeling about the problem and what the objective of the scheduled appointment is.

Start from the problem itself, without deepening into technical odontoiatric aspects. The patient is not interested in implantology just for the sake of it: he just wants to be able to smile again, eat again and so on.

12: GET CONTACT DETAILS

Even if you don't manage to schedule an appointment with the caller, it is very important to collect his personal details (name and email address). If a person calls, it means she/he is interested in the clinic's services. Collect the email address like this:

"[NAME], could you provide us with your email address, so we can send you some useful information and help you decide what the best choice is for you?"

They are rarely reluctant to give the email address, and with such information you can activate other systems in order to acquire the potential patient anyway.

13: IS IT REALLY OVER?

The end of the call should always be like:

"Is there anything else I can do for you?"

followed by heartfelt thanks for the call.

14: CONFIRM OR REMIND?

The words "confirm" and "remind" have different meanings and should be used accordingly! In particular, after you book and schedule an appointment for the patient, the appointment is "confirmed", and afterwards you tell the patient that she/he will be called the day before the appointment to "remind" him. This has a psychological effect...if you call him the day before to "confirm" the appointment, the patient will feel free to cancel it without hesitation!

15: CREATE POSITIVE ANCHORS

Let's take a look together at the structure of a call. The beginning of the call differs, depending whether the call is incoming or outgoing.

Incoming call

- "Thank you for calling [NAME OF THE CLINIC]. How can I help you today?".
- After receiving the the answer, the first thing to ask is "With whom I have the pleasure of speaking?".
- If not already clear, understand if the caller is already a client of the clinic with "How long since your last visit?".

Outgoing call

- Make sure to take a thorough look at the medical records of the patient before the call.
- Dial the number and start off with "Good morning / good afternoon, I am [NAME] calling from [NAME OF THE CLINIC], am i speaking with [NAME OF THE PATIENT]?".
- After the patient confirms, continue with "How are you [NAME OF THE PATIENT]? It's a pleasure to talk to you! Do you have a couple of minutes for me?" NEVER say "May I disturb you?" you are not disturbing anyone, the call is in the interest of the patient.

After the intro, dive into the heart of the call

- Get in sync and make Questions.
- Establish Authority.
- Offer an appointment (taking the circumstance for granted).
- Handle objections, if any (how many just straight out ask: how much does it cost?)
- Offer an appointment again.
- Make a recap of the call and repeat details of the appointment (this way, the patient will feel she/he has been listened to and understood).
- Confirm the appointment and explain an email or a call will reach the patient one day before the appointment as a reminder.
- If an appointment has not been scheduled, make sure to take note of email address.

- End with "Thank you very much for calling [NAME OF THE PATIENT]! Is there anything else I can do for you?".

Handling of objections

- It is very common during a sale to receive objections to your questions, or simply "I will think about it" after offering an appointment. If such were the case, never feel undeterred.

Technical and difficult questions

- In case you receive questions you have no answer for, explain that you will speak with the doctor, who will contact the patient as soon as possible. Take not of the question for the doctor. An answer for the patient, even very short, even my email or text, will have an incredible effect (think about it, who ever does that?). It is important that these mechanism are automated, meaning that every day 5-10 minutes must be dedicated to sending emails with answers for the patients.

Dental care reminder call

- The call as a reminder for dental cleaning or a simple check is fundamental in keeping the patients of the clinic. A good rule should be that the patient should not be let go without scheduling an appointment in the following 6-12 months, even if for a simple check. Not everyone will schedule the appointment and, in such case, the patient's name will join the list of patient to be called periodically.

The reminder call begins as shown before, and goes on as follows:

- Use some "intelligence" and notes about the patient, if any, to get in sync with the patient. For example, ask how was the vacation at the Maldives, is the dog doing well, and so no. (please note: this kind of interactions about the patients' personal lives has an incredible effect, try yourself! And it is currently being used in the UK and the USA. Obviously, you will not find a single underperforming clinic using these techniques).
- Ask if everything is fine with the work done so far, mentioning the latest works (dental implant, dental capsule and so on).
- INVITE, on behalf of the doctor, for a dental hygiene visit, as the visit is due
- If the patients does not want to schedule the appointment, go with a downsell, offering a 30 minutes free dental check, for a control of the latest works and to avoid losing the guarantee.

- ○ If he rejects even the last offer, firmly ask if he intends to remain a patient of the clinic, or if he prefers to close the dental records.

16: "PRICE QUOTATION HUNTERS"

Looking at the statistics, this kind of call happens, even multiple times per day.

For many potential patients, the most immediate way to choose a dental treatment is looking at the prices.

Remember, the only objective is: <u>schedule the appointment</u>

Regardless of the question or the objection of the caller, kindly guide him towards understanding that scheduling an appointment is the best choice to improve the patient's health and smile.

17: EDUCATE THE PATIENT

Try to avoid mentioning the price on the phone - concentrate, instead, on the education of the patient. <u>Help the patient understand that there are plenty of elements to take into account when defining the price of a service</u> (for example, dental implant, dental crown, dental plate and so on).

If the patient insists, only provide a price range.

Always repeat that the best way to know precisely the price for the treatment is to schedule an appointment with the doctor, who will then be able to calculate the works to be done to the exact specification, needs and desires of the patient, helping her/him to stay in the budget range.

Conclusion

Whether or not you agree with the information in this book is of little importance. What will change your professional and personal lives are the actions you take after reading it.

In the last 10 years, technology has changed the way we live and work. Self-driving cars, augmented reality, robots, multi-space rockets. It looks like a sci-fi novel but here they are.

The reason Blockbuster is now ancient history is that people prefer to watch Netflix. If you don't want to be ancient history, you must acknowledge people want to be treated by health professionals who take advantage of technology at all levels.

People prefer to be treated by health professionals who, thanks to digital marketing, are always at the front of their minds. Once you've reached this position, your prospective clients don't want to be bothered any more or even evaluate other solutions. You're done.

The coming years will see robots executing implantology and most surgery treatments. This is where the industry is going. Opening your eyes too late can cause you to lose what you have carefully built over the last years. Waking up too late, placing this book in your library, and focusing only on your usual weekly tasks is a dangerous choice.

At patient-acquisition.com we develop tech solutions that help health professionals take advantage of the revolution that will change their profession.

The first consultation is usually $250 an hour, but we are offering it free to those who have bought and read this book. Reserve your space by writing to us at info@patient-acquisition.com. You'll be asked to fill out a form that pre-evaluates your situation.

During the call, you'll learn about some of our success stories from around the world. We have acquired patients for clinics, hospitals, companies and health professionals.

I hope you enjoyed this book and I wish to help you acquire more and more patients. If you're a great professional, you deserve more patients and they deserve to be treated by you or your staff.

Max Arnaudo

Book References

Chapter 5

The Guardian: *"Teens are abandoning Facebook in dramatic numbers, study finds"* and *"Is Facebook for old people? Over 55s flock in as the young leave."* You'll find links to these articles at the end of this book, among the references.

See Gary V.'s book, Jab Jab, Right Hook, *for the importance of creating marketing content that is not geared toward making a direct sale on your product*

Chapter 7

Medicom Health - *https://medicomhealth.com/*

Chris Boyer - *https://twitter.com/chrisboyer*

Press Ganey - *http://www.pressganey.com/*

Chapter 8

On Porn Addiction - *https://nypost.com/2017/02/16/is-watching-porn-harmful-to-your-health/*

Al Ries and Jack Trout's - *"The 22 laws of marketing"* will offer a clear understanding of this positioning concept.

Smart Marketer by Ezra Firestone - *https://smartmarketer.com/*

Chapter 9

Dr. Joseph A. Gaeta - *Public Awareness In Implant Dentistry: How To Double Your Implant Patients In 60 Days Or Less Through Public Awareness*

Chapt 10

Guy Debord - *La Société du Spectacle*